THREE GIFTS OF THÉRÈSE OF LISIEUX

Three Gifts of
THÉRÈSE OF LISIEUX

A Saint for Our Times

Patrick Ahern

IMAGE

NEW YORK

Published in the United States by Image, an imprint of the Crown
Publishing Group, a division of Random House LLC, a Penguin
Random House Company, New York.
www.crownpublishing.com

IMAGE is a registered trademark, and the "I" colophon is a
trademark of Random House LLC

Library of Congress Cataloging-in-Publication Data
Ahern, Patrick V.
Three gifts of Thérèse of Lisieux: a saint for our times/
Patrick Ahern.—First Edition.
    p.   cm.
1. Thérèse, de Lisieux, Saint, 1873–1897. I. Title.
BX4700.T5A73 2014
282.092—dc23   2013008544

ISBN 978-0-385-34789-1
eBook ISBN 978-0-385-34790-7

PRINTED IN THE UNITED STATES OF AMERICA

Jacket design: Nupoor Gordon
Cover photographs: Shutterstock

1   3   5   7   9   10   8   6   4   2

First Edition

CONTENTS

At first glance, Patrick Ahern and Thérèse of Lisieux might strike most people as an odd couple. Ahern was born and raised in New York City. He rose quickly through the ranks of the priesthood to become secretary to Francis Cardinal Spellman of the Archdiocese of New York during the tumultuous 1960s. It was a position that put him front and center on such issues as the Vietnam War and the civil rights movement, as well as taking him around the world to assist Spellman who was the apostolic vicar for the U.S. Armed Forces. Company for dinner often included the likes of General William Westmoreland and Chiang Kai-shek, the latter serving then as president of China but from the island of Taiwan.

Ahern was by nature witty and gregarious. Often the life of the party, he entertained guests by singing Irish tunes or opera lyrics. At Spellman's request, he once sang for Bob Hope while they were waiting in an airport for their flight. Hope quipped that Ahern was the only "morning lounge singer" he had ever heard. Ahern was also known for striking up conversations with strangers on the street, something he thoroughly enjoyed as much as his encounters with political leaders and great artists.

But more important, he took to heart the people under his care—the families in his parish as well as the hungry, homeless, and abandoned. As pastor—and in 1970 as bishop—he embraced his responsibilities locally and within the American church enthusiastically. It was he who led the local Catholic churches and community leaders to launch the Northwest Bronx Community and Clergy Coalition in the mid-1970s. The coalition became the voice for community revitalization, leading to the creation or renovation of tens of thousands of units of affordable housing to replace the apartment buildings that had been lost through abandonment, vandalism, and arson.

In a later post on Staten Island, he listened to parents who told him of their frustrations caring for their children with special needs, including Down syndrome and autism. They felt the Church offered little assistance, and, wanting to help, he founded the Seton Foundation for Learning. The result was the institution of a group of schools that today educates developmentally disabled children from Staten Island, Manhattan, and Brooklyn from nursery school through high school and beyond.

Thérèse, on the other hand, was so shy and reticent that she was pulled from boarding school and tutored at home as a child. Except for one pilgrimage to Rome with her sister and father, she lived most of her brief life in the small French town of Lisieux, and died at age twenty-four in a cloistered convent she had joined nine years earlier. In the convent her life was "uneventful." The other sisters could not think of anything significant she had done and didn't know what to write in her obituary. It was only after her death that her spiritual autobiography—which she wrote at the request of her superiors—became known. It was well received in other Carmelite convents and shared with family and friends. Word of her work spread rapidly, and two thousand copies of the published book, *The Story of a Soul,* sold out quickly. Her autobiography led to her worldwide popularity.

What drew this well-established priest to this saint from the time he was in the seminary? When asked to preach, more often than not he included a story about her—whether he was speaking before a group of adolescents he was about to confirm, addressing priests and nuns on retreat, or saying Mass at the local parish where he lived. He learned French in his seventies so he could bypass translations and read Thérèse's original writings and the new books written about her by French scholars. He was one of the leading proponents of her being named a Doctor of the Church and personally presented this cause to Pope John Paul II.

Ahern was on the altar with Pope John Paul II in Rome in 1997 when the pope conferred this title on Saint Thérèse almost to the day of the hundredth anniversary of her death. She was only the third woman to hold this title. Recently, a fourth woman, Saint Hildegard of Bingen, was declared a Doctor of the Church. In his retirement Ahern continued to pursue his interest in Thérèse, and in 1998 his book *Maurice and Thérèse: The Story of a Love* was published. It is about Thérèse's friendship with a young unknown priest, Maurice Bellière. Writing it, Ahern said, only solidified his love for her and led to more talks and sermons about her, and eventually to this book, which tells his own story as a priest at the same time as it tells the story of Thérèse.

To Ahern, Thérèse was part of the modern world,

no stranger to its stresses or to the wonder and possibilities that it held. He often referred to her as "a
saint for our times," and this universal appeal was
first of the three gifts she gave us. She was ordinary;
she was one of us. We know about her pet dog, her
family life, her relationship with her sisters and uncle
and cousins, her desires and dreams. We know what
annoyed her, what tempted her, and we know about
the doubts that shook the faith that had sustained
her for as long as she could remember. Thérèse was
accessible, and Ahern never grew tired of rereading
her autobiography. He found strength and guidance
in her words.

In the first section of this book, Ahern describes
the losses Thérèse endured as a child and the psychological toll these traumas took on her. Ahern
believed the sequence of events in her early childhood is pivotal to understanding both her behavior
as a child and also her relevance today. Putting the
pieces together with the understanding afforded him
by contemporary psychology, he goes beyond link-
ing her extreme sensitivity to her mother's death
when she was four. He clarifies what he believes
was the true source of the struggles that she strove
to overcome and finally did when she was thirteen
years old.

Ahern was clearly attuned to the psychological impact of childhood events. His father was an alcoholic, although he provided for his family and saw to it that his sons were raised well. Ahern, ever respectful and loyal, took over his care after his mother died in 1948, visiting him daily in a Carmelite nursing home during the last few years of his life. But it was a relationship that caused him a great deal of pain and resentment. If Thérèse grew up in a home with tremendous loss but always love, Ahern was left with memories that were the source of tremendous insecurities. "How could you be so stupid?" was the question he recalled his father badgering him with. His mother tried to offset episodes that she knew left their mark on her two sons. When she saw Patrick in the morning looking downcast, she would try to cheer him up by saying, "I see Larry on your back. I am going to get him." "Larry" was her term to describe whatever was troubling him. Often she could raise the spirits of her youngest child and make up for her husband's lapses—but not always. His spirit and his confidence were often undermined, he would later admit.

Although each part of this book opens with a personal story, Ahern does not mention his father's alcoholism. He did not like tell-all memoirs that trample on the dead. It is hoped that knowing the basis for his insecurities will help readers to understand more deeply this well-loved bishop and also help readers who share a similar past.

Ahern was drawn to the conviction of Thérèse, the second gift he identifies. He writes about her confidence, which was rooted in her belief that "God is love." It was this love that infused her faith—not the bureaucracy, the rules and commandments, the practices and penances that dominated the Church at that time. Ahern, like so many others, saw an authenticity in Thérèse that spoke to everything he believed about God and wanted for his faith and his Church. "She convinced me that someone as ordinary as I could aspire to the love of God, which filled her heart to overflowing," he writes. This spirit—this love that was so evident in Thérèse—is what he wanted to capture and share with others.

But it was Thérèse's third gift, her Little Way, that firmly anchored Ahern in his own journey, what he described as "her doctrine of littleness, of joyous and wholehearted acceptance of ourselves with all our diminishments, no matter what they are—being glad that we are who we are and have what we have . . .

What she taught us to do was simply to love life the way it is and ourselves the way we are, to love what she called our 'littleness.'"

This doctrine kept him centered in the love of God, and that is why Chapter Eight, "An Unfinished Symphony," was so important to him. It was his hope that any new edition of *The Story of a Soul* would include a second letter Thérèse had written to her sister Marie during her last retreat in which she clarified her spiritual path, "the little way." Ahern believed this second letter was one of her best explanations that little souls like him needed to know.

Marie was always honest. She admitted that she had neither her sister's love of Jesus nor the desire for such love. When Marie asked Thérèse what she was supposed to do in order to love Jesus the way Thérèse did, Ahern recognized she was speaking for us all. He included the full text of this exchange of letters in this book, completing the symphony of the Little Way.

Ahern was fond of quoting Thérèse: "All is grace." As the introduction to each section of this book shows, his deep desire to be a priest was strong, and he was fortunate to have found Thérèse at the start of his priesthood. He worked hard at settling a churning inside him, and constantly went deeper into his faith. He did not hide from painful realities; he was too honest for that. He confronted his fears and lingering feelings of self-doubt. He made friends with his demons. In striving to live authentically, he learned for himself what Thérèse meant by letting go of the past and future and living in the here and now—the present moment. "By the grace of God we are what we are," says Paul.

The last chapter, "The Present Moment," is the story of acceptance and then moving forward.

Soon after completing this book in July 2007 until his death on March 19, 2011, Ahern was confined to a wheelchair and moved to the Carmelite-run Mary Manning Walsh Nursing Home in New York City. He befriended the other residents and those who cared for him with his usual warmth and joy right until the end. He endured the loss of his autonomy with acceptance and often with remarkable good humor. But he was also frequently frustrated and sometimes bored. Accustomed to doing things when he wanted, he had to depend totally on others for everything. He had to learn to be patient, and he had to learn a new kind of acceptance of the present moment. Across from his bed hung an enlarged photograph of

Thérèse. He would gaze out the window or up at the photo and remember that "all is grace," and he would grow peaceful again. Sensing in January 2011 that he was dying, he became more content to be silent in the present moment. But he also agreed with a parishioner who once told him, "Dying is not for sissies." He could not deny the truth of this statement. He died on March 19, 2011, forty-one years to the day of his ordination as a bishop.

As a final note we would like to especially thank the editor Trace Murphy who first championed this book many years ago. Thank you, Trace, not only for helping to shape this book but also for ushering *Maurice and Thérèse: The Story of a Love* from its earliest draft to the final book. We would also like to thank Gary Jansen, senior editor at Image Books at the Crown Publishing Group. Gary, we are forever grateful that when Trace passed on the baton, you assumed the role with equal care and sensitivity. We would also like to extend our appreciation to Claudia Volkman and Maggie Carr for their contributions to the manuscript.

Angela Iadavaia-Cox and Margaret Peet,
November 4, 2011

AUTHOR'S NOTE

When Doubleday, now Image Books, asked me to write a second book about Saint Thérèse of Lisieux, I was delighted. In the first one, I told the inspiring story of her friendship with Maurice Bellière, a troubled priest turned missionary. Afterward Doubleday thought readers might like to know about my own relationship with Thérèse: why I consider her so important and what role she has played in my priesthood of sixty-five years plus. I welcomed with gratitude the chance to take on this project.

Thérèse has been such a presence in my adult life—it is as if I have known her personally; she is as real and alive to me as my lifelong friends. Now, well into my eighties, I have come to understand and appreciate the influence of Thérèse even more. I've identified three gifts that Thérèse has given me, which I would like to offer in this book to everyone seeking to find more meaning in their faith and their journey to find God: her Universal Appeal, her Conviction, and her Little Way.

The Gift of Thérèse's Universal Appeal

I was born and raised in New York City on the West Side of Manhattan. My parents, who came from Ireland, met and married there. They were good people who practiced their religion in an ordinary but earnest way. As members of Blessed Sacrament Parish, they attended Mass each week at its Gothic-style church on Seventy-First Street near Broadway. Neither my mother nor my father ever thought of missing Mass on Sunday or eating meat on Friday, two hallmarks of Catholicism in those days. They expected my brother, Dan, and me to follow their example. In the worst days of the Great Depression, they scraped together the tuition to put us through Catholic grammar school and high school.

In grammar school I applied myself diligently and did well, graduating second in my class, but high school proved to be a different story. School became boring. After freshman year I lost interest in studying and dropped from the top of the class to the bottom. I was two years younger than my classmates, which in retrospect might have inclined me to show off as being wiser than I was. I fell in with the wrong companions on the West Side—or rather, they fell in with me. My adolescence was stormy on all fronts. I thought I was having a good time, but in fact I was miserable for those three years. That stretch of my life was wild and wasteful, and it gives me little pleasure to remember it. But something happened toward the end of senior year. It was trivial enough on the surface, but its effect was profound and it set my life off on a new course.

St. Agnes, the high school I attended on East Forty-Fourth Street, was an old-fashioned school built at the turn of the nineteenth century. It had none of the amenities high schools have today. There was no campus, no gym, no auditorium, no cafeteria. Students brought their lunch in a brown bag and ate it in the classroom, and after lunch they would take a walk through the neighborhood.

On Ash Wednesday of 1935, John Redden, a classmate, and I took one of those walks and passed by a candy store on the corner of Forty-Fourth Street and Lexington Avenue. As we rounded the corner, John asked me to wait while he bought some candy. Im-

pulsively I questioned his eating candy during Lent.
(With all the nonsense going on in my life, I was still
giving up candy for Lent.) John simply replied that
instead of giving up candy he was going to Mass and
Communion every day.

I still remember how foolish I felt, how my face
turned red with a surge of hot blood. I hoped John
did not notice—and I don't think he did, for we
walked on as if nothing had happened. But something *had* happened, something that really stung
me. I anguished over my stupidity. John lived in the
north of the Bronx, near the last stop on the Broadway subway. To get to the eight o'clock Mass at St.
Agnes, he took the Broadway subway at seven from
242nd Street. In those days fasting from midnight
on was required before receiving Holy Communion.
When Mass ended, John hurried across to Nedick's
on Forty-Second Street for the three-for-a-dime
breakfast of orangeade, coffee, and donuts and then
hustled back to school for his first class at eight-forty.
And I, the head wise guy in the class, was giving up
candy.

Humiliation rankled me all afternoon, and that
night I was quiet at supper. When it was time for bed,
I asked my mother to call me early so that I could go
to Mass during Lent. With a mother's wisdom, she

made no remark even though what I proposed to do was quite out of character. I went to sleep listening to the click of the key in the Big Ben clock as she wound it and set the alarm. The next morning she shook me awake at six-thirty and said, without comment, "You said you wanted to go to Mass for Lent." Yes, I replied, got up and dressed, and walked the four blocks to church.

Everything about that walk—the cool of the morning, the empty streets so quiet, even the garbage cans at the curb, which somehow seemed beautiful—is as vivid as if it took place yesterday. I remember how good I felt, and how much I enjoyed Mass. I recall the deep religious fervor I experienced, which increased as Lent went on. I had never had such a reaction to Mass.

After the seven weeks were over I continued to go each day, and daily Mass became the habit of a lifetime. I can count on one hand the times I have missed since that second day of Lent in 1935. For Christmas Mom and Pop gave me a Daily Missal with the Latin on one side and the English on the other. I soon could follow the Mass in Latin, and I recall the sense of achievement this gave me. I no longer feel the fervor of those youthful days, but conviction has taken its place. I would not miss weekday

Mass for anything in the world. Moreover, I think I would not be a priest today if it had not been for John Redden and his nickel bar of candy. Many years went by before I did a little research and found to my amazement that in 1935 Ash Wednesday fell on March 7. Thursday, March 8 was my sixteenth birthday, the first time I ever attended weekday Mass.

When I finished high school I went to work as a mail room clerk in the main office of the W. T. Grant Company. Although I kept up daily Mass, two years passed before I thought of the priesthood. Out of the blue it struck me: Why wouldn't I become a priest? I banished the thought as unfeasible because my former life had been far from what one might expect from a candidate for the priesthood. But the idea soon came back, and this time I entertained it. I talked to a priest whom I liked in my parish, and he encouraged me to give the priesthood a try. I went to college, did very well, and in 1939 I entered St. Joseph's Seminary in Yonkers, New York, still wondering how all this had happened.

A few months into my first year at seminary, something else critically important occurred: I encountered Saint Thérèse. Faculty members took turns giving conferences on Thursday nights, and one night John Middleton, a priest who taught philosophy, spoke eloquently about her. He persuaded me to read her autobiography, *Story of a Soul*. No book has ever had the effect on me that this one did. From cover to cover it was authentic. It spoke to my needs as if it were written with me in mind. Then and there Thérèse became the saint among saints for me, the chief architect of whatever bit of spirituality I have.

Thérèse had a special love for priests and a desire to help them, and the thought that she would support me encouraged me to pursue the priesthood without fear. She opened up a new world for me and made me feel like someone who was grown up. "Confidence and nothing but confidence"[1] was her motto, and confidence was what I needed, not in myself but in God—a strong faith that He could use even me, with all my shortcomings, for whatever He wished to accomplish. Everything I read in her autobiography was reassuring to me and has remained so. I was certain her book was a well of wisdom that would never run dry, and I have not been disappointed. The book

---

1   Thérèse to Sister Marie of the Sacred Heart (Marie), Sept. 17, 1896, in *Letters of St. Thérèse of Lisieux,* vol. 2, 1890–1897, General Correspondence, trans. John Clarke (Washington, D.C.: Institute of Carmelite Studies, 1988), p. 1000; hereafter cited as *Letters,* vol. 2.

is as fresh today as when I first read it at the age of twenty.

I don't mean to imply that the teaching and example of Saint Thérèse launched me on an untroubled life. My life has never stayed untroubled for long. It has been up and down all the way, with slips and falls, highs and lows, real disappointments with myself, difficult times painful to remember, and episodes I wish had never happened. But for me, one thing that has never changed is my enthusiasm for Thérèse. Her spirituality is realistic and achievable, always with encouragement for improvement and with patience when that improvement is slow in coming. Thérèse was never one to badger or to nag. There is only one thing she did not tolerate, and that was discouragement. There is no room for it in her theology of the Little Way. I have found her a true and loyal friend, who has traveled the long road with me, neither inspiring false sympathy nor allowing me to languish in self-recrimination. She has always been there for me in times of crisis, and her words and life remain a constant and gracious encouragement and presence for me.

I am not alone in this perception of Thérèse nor in having benefited from her having had a central place in my life.

CHAPTER 1

The Wounded Psyche

Few saints have enjoyed the widespread appeal of Saint Thérèse of Lisieux. In the century since her death she has become known and loved throughout the world. Abbé Combes, the author of several highly regarded studies on her, often spoke of her as "the Universal Saint."

What accounts for such popularity? What makes so many—from scholars to the poorest of poor, from artists to monks—find inspiration in this woman who lived to only twenty-four years old? For me the answer is simple: She captures many hearts because she is so completely, warmly human. People relate to her experiences, which we know about in detail from her own writings and those of her contemporaries, especially her sisters. In her autobiography she reveals personal secrets, which few are so candid to admit. She tells us that she was powerfully drawn to God as a little child, but she also tells us about her struggles growing up and her painful adolescence. She was said to be a stubborn child and impatient, yet also reflective. In the twenty-four short years of her life she reached the heights of spiritual development while struggling not only with the darkest of spiritual nights but also with the physical pain of illness and the frustrations of living with a group of women. To know Thérèse is to understand that she is one of us. Within the parameters of her family life and then life in the convent, she is a saint within our reach.

In reading her account of her childhood, we learn that a good part of her early years was marked by an excessive sensitivity, which she did not overcome until she was thirteen years old. She showed uncommon courage in struggling with this tendency, but the problem persisted and wreaked havoc on her. She was much too easily hurt, often cried, blushed unaccountably, felt shy with strangers, and found it hard to compete with other children. Although she was very bright, she had to be taken out of school and placed with a tutor, lest the pressure prove too much for her and cause a nervous breakdown. She admits all this in her autobiography with disarming candor. Speaking of when she was thirteen, she writes:

I was really unbearable because of my extreme touchiness; if I happened to cause anyone I loved some little trouble, even unwittingly, instead of forgetting about it and not *crying*, which made matters worse, I *cried* like a Magdelene and then when I began to cheer up, I'd begin *to cry again for having cried*. All arguments were useless; I was quite unable to correct this terrible fault. I really don't know how I could entertain the thought of entering Carmel [the convent] when I was still in the *swaddling clothes of a child*!

God would have to work a little miracle to make me *grow up* in an instant.[2]

What caused such behavior were the psychological wounds of maternal loss she experienced in childhood. When a child is very young, such a loss can shake his or her sense of security. Thérèse suffered this loss not once but five times. Although she grew up surrounded by love in a splendid family, a series of sudden separations left her at sea emotionally.

Thérèse was born into a deeply religious family.

---

2 *Story of a Soul: The Autobiography of St. Thérèse of Lisieux,* 3rd ed., trans. John Clarke (Washington, D.C.: Institute of Carmelite Studies, 1996), p. 97; hereafter cited in the text as *Story*.

Her parents married late in life because they both first considered joining religious communities. Louis Martin felt drawn to the contemplative life and applied for admission to a Cistercian monastery in the Alps, but after serious deliberation he abandoned the idea and instead trained to become a watchmaker. Zélie Guérin, for her part, had an earnest wish to serve the poor in the Sisters of the Hôtel Dieu in Alençon, but after lengthy discussions with their superior she reached the conclusion that she was meant for marriage and raising a family. She took up the art of hand making the famous lace of Alençon. When Louis and Zélie met, each was the owner of a small business—he of a prosperous jewelry shop in town and she of a thriving lacemaking enterprise in the same town.

The story of their first encounter is quite romantic. They met while crossing a bridge one morning on their way to work. They had seen each other before, but on this occasion their eyes lingered in mutual admiration. He arranged to be introduced to her formally, and within three months they were married. Clearly they were meant for each other, and their marriage became a remarkable success.

The Martins were the parents of nine children, three of whom died in infancy and one at the age of eight. The five remaining girls were Marie, Pauline, Léonie, Céline, and Thérèse. As the youngest of the siblings, Thérèse was also the darling of the family. She had joyous memories of her early childhood. Zélie's letters to her older daughters, who were at boarding school during much of this time, are filled with charming anecdotes about their baby sister. She was the prettiest of them all, the happy mother did not hesitate to report. She was gay and quick to learn, outgoing and affectionate, although with a mind of her own. She was "the little imp" and the joy of the family, her mother would say. Thérèse would recall these years fully appreciative of the love she received. "God was pleased all through my life to surround me with *love,* and the first memories I have are stamped with smiles and the most tender caresses," she later wrote (*Story,* p. 17).

The Loss of Her Mother

When Thérèse was almost four, Zélie discovered she had breast cancer, and she died six months later. In her autobiography, Thérèse describes the family kneeling at her deathbed, her father bent over with his face in his hands, sobbing. She tells us that, surprisingly, she herself did not cry; nor did she cry when the coffin was brought in and placed outside her mother's bedroom door. She stood before it lost in thoughtful silence, knowing it would carry Mama's body away and she would never see her again. It was too much for tears for her. This once joyous and lively child was suddenly quiet and withdrawn. She was entering what she would later call the second period of her life, and the most painful. She became overly sensitive and shy, making her experience at school in a few years very difficult.

Thérèse's relationship with her sister Pauline was especially important at this time. When the family came home from the funeral the maid—with intended sympathy but little tact—said to her, "Poor little things, you have no mother any more!" Thérèse bounded into Pauline's arms and exclaimed: "It's Pauline who will be my Mama!" (*Story*, p. 34). The two at once formed a relationship that became very strong. Ten years older than Thérèse, Pauline in truth became her mother: said her prayers with her each day, got her dressed in the morning, supervised her education, and put her to bed at night, kissing her fondly as she fell asleep.

The two shared all their secrets. Pauline confided to her that she would one day enter the Carmelite convent on the other side of town. Thérèse had often passed it on walks and was full of questions about the nuns behind the walls. She told Pauline that she would enter too. Though she was only a child when she said this, she never doubted that her vocation could be traced back to her childhood, not simply to follow Pauline but because of her own desire to give her life to Jesus so totally.

The Loss of Pauline

When Thérèse was ten she was shocked to overhear Pauline telling Marie, the oldest in the family and now the manager of the household, that she was ready to enter Carmel and would do so very soon. This grievously wounded Thérèse, though she mentioned it to no one—least of all to Pauline. She kept it to herself for years until she wrote her autobiography when she was twenty-two, a book not written on her own initiative but under obedience to her prioress in the Carmel convent, who happened to be Pauline at the time. In her autobiography she remarked that what hurt her most was not Pauline's departure, but that she broke the news to Marie without first telling her. For a time there were feelings of estrangement from Pauline, which made Thérèse's second maternal loss more difficult to handle.

Not long after Pauline's departure, Thérèse had a serious breakdown, an indication of how deeply attached she was to her sister. She was bedridden for eight weeks. Her conduct became bizarre, and she suffered hallucinations. A nail on the wall became a serpent, her father's black hat an object of terror. She thrashed about wildly in bed and banged her head against the bedposts. Doctors were unable to diagnose this illness. Thérèse herself suspected diabolic possession, and later in life she spoke of what she felt was the devil's part in it. While it is not possible to be sure of the true nature of the sickness, it would be unwise to brush aside her suspicion, for she was extremely bright and psychologically perceptive. Whatever it was, Thérèse was no stranger to suffering, as we shall later see.

It came to the point that the family feared they would lose her, and they prayed desperately for her cure. The girls brought a statue of the Virgin Mary into her room and begged her for a miracle. Suddenly and mysteriously Thérèse was restored to health. Marie, who had assumed the role of mother after

Pauline left for the cloister, was with her at the time and noticed that Thérèse was staring at the statue just as the cure occurred. Later she asked Thérèse what she had seen. Thérèse did not reply, but Marie persisted: "Do tell me what you saw."

Reluctantly she answered that she had seen the Virgin smile and that her smile was "ravishing." The words were hardly spoken when she regretted them, feeling she had no right to divulge what should have been left a secret. Marie told Pauline, who told the nuns in Carmel, and the story quickly traveled through Lisieux.

Thérèse was mortified, another example of her sensitivity. First she blamed herself for revealing what she felt she should have kept to herself. Then she began to question whether she actually saw the Virgin smile. Finally she wondered if she had invented the entire episode: the cure and even the illness itself, just to get attention for herself. Could the whole experience have been a figment of her imagination? How complex her mind was at the age of ten, and how prone she was to question the existence of a miracle! She lived with this state of perplexity for four years until, while visiting the Church of Notre-Dame des Victoires, she became sure that the Virgin had smiled at her and her illness had not been some sort of unconscious ruse. As she prayed in this church before the statue, the doubt quietly went away and never came back.

The Loss of Marie

Further trials were in store for Thérèse. At the age of twelve, a critical time for a growing girl, she developed a case of scrupulosity, a not uncommon anxiety neurosis that afflicts a person with feelings of guilt about things that do not reflect any wrongdoing or sin on his or her part. In Thérèse's case the scruples had to do with sexual images, which kept invading her imagination the more she tried to dispel them. In all simplicity she revealed them to her confidante, Marie, who dismissed them as nonsense. The advice pacified her troubled conscience, but only temporarily. She kept coming back to Marie with the same worry—seesawing is a typical feature of scruples.

In the midst of this crisis, Marie, who was the last person anyone would think would enter a convent, felt called by God to Carmel. She did not for a moment question the call, and she did not delay in answering it. Within a few weeks she joined Pauline in Carmel, where she played a very important role in the mission of Thérèse.

Once again Thérèse was devastated by maternal loss, left with no one in whom she could confide her delicate dilemma. Her scruples persisted, and she turned in desperation to her four little brothers and sisters who had died when their lives had hardly begun. She reminded them that she was their youngest sister and she had no one else to help her. She pleaded for their help. Shortly thereafter, without anything dramatic occurring, the scruples quietly disappeared, although her sensitivity would continue to afflict her, as she later would write.

It should now be clear that maternal loss was at the root of Thérèse's adolescent feelings of insecurity. But a question inevitably arises. Why was Thérèse so vulnerable to maternal loss that the death of her mother created serious psychological problems that would take ten years to resolve? Others might suffer a similar crisis when they were young without sustaining the damage Thérèse did. Was there something in her background that made her more vulnerable than the average child?

The Very First Loss

In fact, there *was* something that made Thérèse vulnerable to maternal loss, and what it was has not received the attention it deserves. The death of her mother was not her first maternal loss. She had experienced a painful separation twice in her early infancy.

When Thérèse was only three months old she developed serious pulmonary difficulties, which left her struggling for breath and wheezing alarmingly. Her parents were terrified that they would lose her as they had already lost four young children. The family doctor said their fear was well founded. Alençon was a smoky city, and what the baby needed if she was to survive was to be out in the country air for an extended time, in order to give her lungs a chance to heal and recover fully. He urged Louis and Zélie to send her away.

There was a woman named Rose Taillé, a farmer's wife in Semallé, six miles from where the Martins lived. Thérèse could stay with her. Once before, Rose had been helpful when Joseph Martin was ailing as a baby. Regrettably he died, but the Martins knew that this was not because of any neglect on Rose's part. She had done everything possible to nurse him back to health and was heartbroken when he died. Rose had recently given birth to a baby boy, and she would be able to nurse Thérèse.

The difficult decision was taken, and Thérèse was brought to Semallé. That was her first maternal separation, and its devastating impact must not be underestimated. It is hard to measure the effect on a three-month-old child who is taken from her mother's arms and given to a stranger, in a place she has never seen. There was a time when we might have thought that she was only a baby and babies get over shocks like these—they don't even remember them. But we know better now. The shock (we refer to it as trauma today) does not go away. It remains hidden in the psyche, much to the detriment of the child.

The Loss of Rose

Still to come was another such experience, when Thérèse was less than a year and a half old. By this time, life with Rose was delightful. Rose was thrilled to have this wonderful baby girl in her home. She cuddled her and kissed her, laughed into her face, and raised her high in maternal jubilation. She carried Thérèse about the farm as she did the daily chores, feeding the chickens and collecting their eggs, and milking the family's only cow. It was on that farm in Semallé that Thérèse developed her deep love of nature: the chickens, the cow, the fields full of flowers, the white clouds in the sunny sky, the distant views of the hills on the horizon. At night Rose placed her gently in her cradle and sang to her the lullabies she was used to singing to her own children.

Thérèse spent more than a year in Semallé. By then her lungs had cleared and her health was fully restored, and she was ready to be brought home. But, of course, by then she was attached to Rose. Her family had often come for visits, and sometimes Rose brought her to the Martin home in Alençon, but to the little baby they were strangers, delightful people, to be sure, who made a great fuss over her—but Rose was her mother. When Zélie came to take her away, there was a frightening scene. Thérèse screamed when she was torn from Rose's arms and given back to the mother who had brought her into the world.

I once visited the Martin home in Alençon where two nuns were caretakers. The house stands on the main road leading into town. One of the sisters told me something I have never been able to forget. A story survives in Alençon that Rose Taillé on occasion passed the house, pushing a cart of produce from the farm to the market in the center of town. If Thérèse happened to be looking out the window and saw her, she would burst into tears. "Can you imagine," asked the nun, "what this did to her mother?" But the real question is what it did to Thérèse. It took some time for this little child to realize who her mother was—only to suffer her loss, and that of her two sisters, in subsequent years.

Semallé is a very important chapter in the story of Thérèse, more than just a year in a very formative period of her life. The oversensitivity that she experienced in her early years should not be interpreted as the tantrums of a spoiled child. Thérèse was carrying heavy baggage as she entered her fifth year, and growing up from then on would be no easy process, despite all the affection her parents and sisters lavished upon her. When she finally hit her stride at the age of fourteen, she was a poised and valiant woman, who had earned her laurels in the school of hard knocks and was ready for the important mission that God entrusted to her.

CHAPTER 2

Rooted in God's Grace

Although Thérèse's childhood and adolescence were filled with traumatic loss, it would be a great mistake to forget that from her earliest days she was deeply rooted in God and constantly growing in His love. She once told her sister Céline, "I think that from the age of three and a half I have never been more than five minutes without thinking of God." She said that she had never held anything back from Him that she thought He wanted from her. She tells us furthermore that throughout her life, in the worst of times as well as the best, she never lost His peace, which dwelt in the deep interior of her soul.

Her familiarity with God was not visionary or ecstatic but full of the innocence of childhood. She was at home with God. She did not share these experiences with others, except on rare occasions when she broke her silence with her sister Céline, who was the "sister of my soul," as she called her. She was otherwise very private about her interior life, revealing its depths only in the later years when she wrote her autobiography.

Manuscript A, the first part of her autobiography, in which she was requested to recount her childhood, gives us some insight into this relationship with God. Her father, whom she dearly loved, was a gentle man, whose life by and large was tranquil but who had to contend with the pressures of running his jewelry business while at the same time managing the financial aspects of his wife's lacemaking enterprise. One of his diversions was to spend an occasional afternoon fishing at a favorite lake not far from town. Sometimes he took his little girl along for company. It was a special treat to go out to the lake with him. He would fashion a small rod for her from the branch of a tree so she could try her luck at the water's edge, while he rowed out to deeper waters to try his own. Here is a description of one of those treasured afternoons, when she left the fishing to Papa and became lost in her own world.

I preferred to go *alone* and sit down on the grass bedecked with flowers, and then my thoughts became very profound indeed! Without knowing what it was to meditate, my soul was absorbed in real prayer. I listened to distant sounds, the murmuring of the wind, etc. At times, the indistinct notes of some military music reached me where I was, filling my heart with a sweet melancholy. . . .

I remember one day when the beautiful blue sky became suddenly overcast and soon the thunder began to roll and the lightning to flash through the dark clouds. I saw it strike a short distance away, and, far from being frightened, I was thrilled with delight because God seemed to be so close! (*Story*, pp. 37–38)

Hurrying home in the downpour, she asked her father to hold her hand and guide her so that she could look up at the storm and laugh as the rain ran down her face.

This lovely story opens a door for us on the wonderful inner world of her childhood. She was blessed by God with a grace, which would bear abundant fruit in the years to come.

In her autobiography she also recalls a conversation with one of the Benedictine nuns at the abbey school she attended. It took place at the very time she was having troubles in school, doing very well academically but experiencing a hard time mingling with her schoolmates and playing their games.

> One day, one of my teachers at the Abbey asked me what I did on my free afternoons when I was alone. I told her I went behind my bed in an empty space which was there, and that it was easy to close myself in with my bedcurtain and that *"I thought."* "But what do you think about?" she asked. "I think about God, about life, about ETERNITY . . . I *think*!" The good religious laughed heartily at me, and later on she loved reminding me of the time when I *thought*, asking me if *I was still thinking.* I understand now that I was making mental prayer without knowing it and that God was already instructing me in secret. (*Story,* pp. 74–75)

We can't fail to notice the artless candor of her reply to the nun, nor to see that she was already a contemplative with a familiarity with God that was prodigious. "God was already instructing me in secret." She was about nine when this took place. All the emotional turmoil could not slow her progress as a mystic. Nothing could rob her of the deep peace she was finding in her friendship with Jesus.

.   .   .

However, it was Christmas Eve 1886 when, at the age of thirteen, Thérèse was finally able to reconcile her fragile sensitivity with her spiritual awareness. In one unforgettable experience she moved from her flawed adolescence into the maturity of her admirable womanhood.

At the time, only Papa, Céline, and Thérèse were living at home. As the three were leaving the house for midnight Mass, Céline let Papa and Thérèse go first so that she could delay for a second to prepare a surprise for them on their return. She ran over to the fireplace to put Thérèse's slippers there, filled with her Christmas presents. This had been a custom in their childhood, and Céline thought that Papa and Thérèse would have a laugh when they came back from Mass. They would find the presents, as if Santa Claus had come down the chimney with them while his team of reindeer waited on the roof.

For her part, as Thérèse entered their cathedral parish for midnight Mass, one issue alone preoccupied her: She would celebrate her fourteenth birthday on January 2. She had already settled in her mind that her vocation was to Carmel, and moreover she was determined that she would enter once she reached her fifteenth year. On this night, however, she wondered how she could join such a demanding and austere religious order if she was still not in command of her emotions.

After receiving Holy Communion she returned to her pew in church and prayed as she had never prayed before. With her face in her hands, she begged Jesus for the grace to overcome her adolescent sensitivity. What she had not been able to do in ten long years of struggle, she asked Him to do for her as His gift on this Christmas night. She would never forget how she prayed at that moment, with tears rolling down her cheeks. Little did she realize, her prayers were about to be answered. She would soon be able to demonstrate a new strength in matters of the heart both large and small.

When the three returned home from Mass, Papa was the first to enter the house, followed by Céline, and the first thing he saw was the slippers in the fireplace. Instead of being amused by Céline's gesture, he turned to her and sternly remarked: "She's too old for that now. Let this be the last time for the slippers in the fireplace." He did not intend Thérèse to hear what he said, for he knew that such a remark would precipitate her tears. But she did hear, and Céline saw that she did. She followed her sister up the stairs as she went to remove her hat and coat. Taking Thérèse by the shoulders Céline asked her to wait before going down, saying, "You know you'll cry and spoil Christmas for Papa." Thérèse pushed her aside and started down the stairs. She records in her autobiography that her heart was thumping fiercely. She took her slippers to the chair where Papa was sitting. As she opened his presents, her face was radiant, and her eyes were shining with joy. She threw her arms around his neck, thanking him and wishing him Happy Christmas. "Joyeux Noel, Papa!" she exclaimed. Céline could not believe her eyes.

Never again did Thérèse cry over trifles. She put her childhood behind her forever. She always remembered what happened that night and referred to it as "my grace" or "little miracle."

Thérèse later explained the significance of this event. Referring to her great desire to practice virtue as a child, she wrote in her autobiography, "I went about it in a strange way" (*Story*, p. 97). As the youngest in the family with four older sisters, she wasn't accustomed to doing things for herself. So to please God, she would try to do different tasks that she thought would be helpful to others. Unfortunately, she had misplaced expectations about her deeds: "[I]t was for *God alone* I was doing these things and

[I] should not have expected any *thanks* from creatures. Alas, it was just the opposite. If Céline was unfortunate enough not to seem happy or surprised because of these little services, I became unhappy and proved it by my tears" (*Story*, p. 97).

After her Christmas "miracle," however, her focus shifted. "I felt *charity* enter into my soul, and the need to forget myself and to please others; since then I've been happy!" She quoted the apostles: "'Master, I fished all night and caught nothing.' More merciful to me than He was to His disciples, Jesus *took the net Himself,* cast it, and drew it in filled with fish. He made me a fisher of *souls.* I experienced a great desire to work for the conversion of sinners, a desire I hadn't felt so intensely before" (*Story*, pp. 98–99).

Clearly, the ten years between the death of her mother and the Christmas miracle give evidence of her wounded psyche, but this was not a dormant time. The period of psychological stress in her adolescence gave her strength and an understanding of human frailty. We should not be at all astonished that God chose this highly gifted and severely tested child to lead us in the stressful search to find ourselves. As Thérèse came to realize, she was a little soul whose great sanctity would be fashioned from her littleness.

The Gift of Thérèse's Conviction

Midway through my seminary days, doubts about my vocation suddenly assailed me. They struck at a vulnerable moment during a long and lonely winter semester. During Christmas vacation I had suffered a blood clot, which left me with a painful phlebitis in my leg. I could attend classes and morning Mass but had to spend the rest of the day in my room elevating my leg. Two Russian novels helped to pass the time: *War and Peace* and *Crime and Punishment*, assuredly great works of literature but hardly light reading. As my mood darkened, a question stole into my mind: Did I belong in the priesthood? My answer was maybe yes but more likely no.

Discussions with my spiritual director did not help. He had me draw up two columns, one with the reasons that I should stay in the seminary and the other with the reasons that I should leave. This got me nowhere, and I finally told him so. I said I thought that I needed to talk to another priest, one who did not know me—preferably one who was old. (Something told me it was important for him to be old.) He sent me to a Jesuit at Fordham.

Down I went the following Wednesday, which was our weekly free day, to meet Father J. Harding Fisher. His appearance was almost as impressive as his name. He was in his late eighties, but age had left his stunning looks unspoiled. His wavy white hair was neatly groomed, his cheeks were rosy with health, and his deep-set blue eyes were full of kindness. With a welcoming smile he waved me to an easy chair and made me feel at home. After some pleasant small talk, he leaned into the purpose of my visit. "I hear you're having trouble with your vocation," he said. "Tell me about yourself." For nearly an hour I told him all that I thought was significant in my life. While he listened with interest, he said scarcely a word. Then I told him of my frustration with the two columns, listing the reasons why I should go on to the priesthood and why I should give it up.

When I finished, he smiled and said, "Let me tell you what I think. I think you're asking the wrong question: Should you be a priest or not? That's not a real question, and you could never find the answer to it. Let me change the question for you, but I want you to answer either yes or no without any hesitation, whatever comes first to your mind. If your answer is yes, I'll say that's the answer, and if it is no, I'll say the same, and we'll go on from there.

"Here's the question: 'Do you want to be a priest?'"

Spontaneously I replied: "Father, I really do! There is nothing else in the world I really want to be." There was a surge of enthusiasm in my voice.

He laughed and said: "Then that's the answer, and you may be sure it is right. You're a good enough young fellow who will make a fine priest. Go back to the seminary, work hard at your studies, and put your whole heart into your prayers. And *never revisit* the question."

I shall always remember Father Fisher and what he did for me in a single encounter. When I went out through the gates of Fordham, I was walking on top of the clouds. I never revisited the question. I knew I was where I belonged and still do. I wanted to be a priest, and I could commit to my vocation. I would struggle forever to be a good priest, but I never doubted that this was what I wanted to do. In retrospect I can see that by reframing my question Father Fisher was able to get at what was really bothering me: Was I good enough; did I belong? versus what did I want? Father Fisher's more simple and direct question drew a gut response from me, overcoming the lingering sense of guilt that stemmed from my youthful escapades.

At the same time by no means could he wipe away all the negative feelings that had been holding me back. A sense of inadequacy persisted to some extent all my life, frequently dormant, but at other times strong enough to come out of the box to bite me. That day, however, I knew in my heart that I was good enough for God: I wanted to be a priest and I wanted to be a good priest. Father Fisher shifted my focus from guilt over the past to what I wanted to do with my life in the future. I was, of course, ready for this sudden leap. I had gone back and forth long enough within myself to resolve this matter—I was ready to receive the love of God that was always right there waiting for me.

I have no idea whether Father Fisher was a devotee of Saint Thérèse, but I have a strong suspicion that he was. She is many things to many people, but she is especially helpful when it comes to managing feelings, both those that make us want to take on the world and those that keep us from moving forward and render us almost useless. As we have seen, Thérèse was by nature sensitive, and her spiritual life was rich and fervent. In these next three chapters we will look at what truly motivated this young saint— what gave her confidence and conviction in the face of her own desires and her own desolation. The faith she experienced in the Carmelite convent was very different from the inspired faith she had at the time of her Christmas miracle. While she gained the strength to move beyond herself, she would eventually lose the "feeling" of comfort and inspiration her faith had long offered. Instead, Thérèse would rely on her conviction. She would focus her attention on what was most important to her: loving God, saving souls, and simply pushing on, as life often requires of us all.

CHAPTER 3

Walking with the Stride of a Giant

Christmas 1886 was the turning point in Thérèse's life. After that night she said she walked "with the stride of a giant." She entered an extraordinary time of special grace during which she would later write:

> I felt within my heart certain aspirations unknown until then, and at times I had veritable transports of love.
>
> One evening, not knowing how to tell Jesus that I loved Him and how much I desired that He be loved and glorified everywhere, I was thinking He would never receive a single act of love from hell; then I said to God that to please Him I would consent to see myself plunged into hell so that He would be *loved* eternally in that place of blasphemy. . . . [W]hen we love, we experience the

need of saying a thousand foolish things. (*Story*, p. 112)

Her prayers were fervent at this time, deeply felt and satisfying. There is a well-known story of one beneficiary of her prayers, a criminal named Henri Pranzini who was condemned to die for the brutal murder of two women and a child. Thérèse instinctively knew that given the brutality of this incident, it would be Pranzini who needed prayers the most. She was intent on saving his soul, and she devoted her prayers for his salvation. So convinced was she that he would be saved, she asked for a sign that her prayers had been heard. She desired a sign she said "to obtain courage to pray for sinners" and also for "my own simple consolation." She received that sign when she read in the papers how Prazini took hold of the crucifix the priest was holding and "*kissed the sacred wounds three times!*" before dying (*Story*, p. 100).

Thérèse became more sure than ever that she was ready for Carmel. She knew with a new certainty that she wanted to spend her life saving souls. She decided to pursue her vocation against every obstacle that stood in her way. Bishop Hugonin was opposed to this, and so was his vicar general. The priest who represented the bishop at Carmel was adamant in his opposition and bitter in his expression of it. They felt strongly that she was too young to make a lifetime decision. But there was no stopping her. She knew in her heart that she was not too young, that God clearly was calling her, and she had to answer His call without delay. She had always sensed that she would not have a long life, and she felt she had no time to waste. She knew that God was calling her to Carmel, and ever since the night of the Christmas miracle when she became a mature woman, she was convinced that it was His intention that she be in the convent on the following Christmas, which would be one week short of her fifteenth birthday.

At the time when Bishop Hugonin declined permission for Thérèse to enter Carmel at fifteen, a pilgrimage to Rome was being organized in Lisieux to honor the golden jubilee of Pope Leo XIII's ordination as a priest. Her father was eager to join in this occasion, and he offered to bring Thérèse with him. He thought the trip would give her a chance to ask the pope for a dispensation from the age requirement. She gladly accepted his offer, and it was arranged for Céline to make the pilgrimage, too.

In the early morning of November 4 the three took the train for Paris, planning to spend a few days sightseeing and then join the other pilgrims on their way to Rome. We can imagine the excitement of the two young women as they boarded the train in Lisieux to begin their first and only trip abroad. There was much to see in the great city of Paris, with its museums and churches and places of historic interest, but the place Thérèse was most eager to visit was the Church of Notre-Dame des Victoires, where she would be able to see the original of the little statue she had prayed before when she was so ill as a child. She still harbored some uncertainty about whether she had been cured by the smile of Mary or if it had been all her imagination. But as she prayed in the cathedral, Thérèse intuitively knew it had truly been the smile of Mary that she had seen. She writes, "Ah! what I felt kneeling at her feet cannot be expressed. . . . The Blessed Virgin made me feel *it was really herself who smiled on me and brought about my cure.* . . . I could no longer give her any other name but *'Mama,'* as this appeared ever so much more tender than Mother" (*Story,* p. 123). Thérèse was more than ready for her trip to Rome. At last the pilgrims assembled in the Gare de l'Est and made off in high spirits for their anticipated destination.

Thérèse and Céline were enchanted by the scenery as the train wound its way up into the Alps. Thérèse could not get enough of it, and she dashed from one side of their railway car to the other, trying to see it all: the snowcapped peaks, the incredible waterfalls thundering down the mountains, the fertile valleys below with their peaceful flocks grazing on the rich land, farm after farm. She put into the bank of her memory the most beautiful scenes in the world as the train passed through the countryside, promising herself that after the gates of Carmel closed behind her, these scenes would be hers to enjoy forever.

In Rome there was more to be seen: the churches, the ruins of the Eternal City, the catacombs, the Colosseum where the early martyrs suffered. They squeezed all the guided tours they could into their short stay until the day for the papal audience came at last. Thérèse's mind was racing in anticipation. Each pilgrim would kneel before the pope and exchange a few words with him. Unfortunately, some had more words than others, and the aged pope, who was not feeling well that day, began to show signs of fatigue. The Martins were near the end of the line when Monsignor Révérony, the bishop's secretary who had been standing at the pope's side, announced that the remaining pilgrims must not engage the pope in conversation, but instead simply kneel for his blessing and kiss his ring. Shortly after the announcement, Thérèse's big moment arrived. She turned to look at

Céline who was standing behind her, and Céline uttered a single word to her younger sister: "Speak!" (*Story,* p. 134).

Thérèse knelt and took the pope's hand in her own. "Holy Father, in honor of your Jubilee, permit me to enter Carmel at the age of fifteen!" The pope was confused by her request and turned to Monsignor Révérony for help. He replied: "Most Holy Father, . . . this is *a child* who wants to enter Carmel at the age of fifteen, but the Superiors are considering the matter at the moment." The pope said to Thérèse, "Well, my child, . . . do what the Superiors tell you!" She rested her hands on the pope's knees and said: "Oh! Holy Father, if you say yes, everybody will agree!" He responded, "Go . . . go . . . *You will enter if God wills it!*" Two members of the Swiss Guard took hold of her by the arms. When they were lifting her away from the pope, "the Holy Father placed his hand on my lips, then raised it to bless me" (*Story,* pp. 134–35). She left the audience hall in tears.

In 1935 Pauline received a letter from an Italian nun stationed in Egypt that contained a delightful surprise. The nun explained that years ago her father had been a member of the Swiss Guard, and her family lived in Vatican City. One night when she was seven years old he came home from his duties in the papal household and told the family at the dinner table about a beautiful French girl who had implored the pope to be admitted to a Carmel in France even though she was underage. He had tears in his eyes as he told the story, and the family was deeply moved as they listened. When the nun read the account in the autobiography, the book nearly fell from her hands. That girl was the now famous Thérèse.

Pauline must have been deeply moved, too, when she read the story told by an eyewitness who had no idea that the young girl was her sister, nor that Thérèse had written to her as soon as she was back in the hotel room. Thérèse's letter was an impassioned account of what happened and her disappointment. Yet in the middle of the letter she gave a description of the pope, which reflects her humor: "The good pope is so old that one would say he is dead; I would never have pictured him like this."[3] It is easy to imagine a line like that from a typical teenager today.

The journey was a success, however. Monsignor Révérony, far from being annoyed with Thérèse for

---

[3] Thérèse to Sister Agnes of Jesus (Pauline), Nov. 20, 1887, in *Letters of St. Thérèse of Lisieux,* vol. 1, 1877–1890, General Correspondence, trans. John Clarke (Washington, D.C.: Institute of Carmelite Studies, 1982), p. 353; hereafter cited as *Letters, vol. 1.*

disregarding his admonition at the papal audience, had a new admiration for her determination and courage. The way she had behaved with the pope was an eye-opener, and he observed her closely for the remainder of the pilgrimage. This was no hysterical teenager acting out, but a serious young woman whose heart was breaking because sensible people were preventing her from carrying out the will of God. Her deadline was simply not negotiable, and she was obliged to meet it.

Riding along in one of the carriages with Thérèse at his side, Monsignor Révérony leaned over confidentially and told her that when he saw Bishop Hugonin upon arriving home he would speak with him to plead her cause. There was still hope, and Thérèse cherished that hope. He kept his word, and the bishop gave his permission. She was not, however, accepted for entrance in time for Christmas. The convent made its own decision that she must wait until after Lent. It was felt that the rigorous fast the sisters kept for this penitential season would be too much for someone so young.

This was a disappointment, but Thérèse used the time to advantage. She became strict about doing little things for God, performing small courtesies for others, sitting up erect without leaning against the back of a chair, curbing her impatience, and the like. She recalled that she read intently during this period to make up for the time she had lost at school. Her teacher, Madame Papinau, provided her with a number of books, which she read voraciously. It would be interesting to know what they were, but we do not have that information. We know that she was very interested in science and history and that she did read two books—one was Thomas à Kempis's *Imitation of Christ* and the other was Father Charles Arminjon's *End of the Present World and the Mysteries of the Future Life*. Thérèse was very bright and picked up much from her reading.

The night before she entered Carmel, the family shared their last meal together. It was a very moving moment, and those at the table cried, but Thérèse did not shed a tear. They cried again at the Mass the next morning in Carmel, but not Thérèse. When the Mass was over she led the way to the cloister door. She knelt to receive her father's blessing, and then he knelt for hers. She tells us that her heart was pounding. The nuns gave her a tour of the convent and showed her to the cell she would occupy. All she could keep saying to herself over and over was "I am here forever and ever!" (*Story*, p. 148).

CHAPTER 4

The Desert of Carmel

When she walked through the cloister door the day she entered Carmel, Thérèse had no illusions. Nothing surprised or shocked or scandalized her. All the nuns were much older than she was, and some would have liked to make this fifteen-year-old girl the pet of the community, but they stood no chance. She knew who she was, and she knew the grace God gave her. She took the Carmelite rule seriously, determined to let it form her into the fullness of what God wanted her to be. She did not allow her sisters, Marie and Pauline, to hover over her. One day she wrote to Marie expressing how much she meant to her but also acknowledging that they did not enter Carmel to be with one another, but to be with Jesus. It was not easy to say that to her oldest sister, but she meant it, and Marie and Pauline were careful from then on to respect her privacy and not intrude on her adventure with Jesus.

Thérèse kept the rule of silence meticulously— although she was never offended by anyone who broke it. She was a master of diplomacy. Others would hardly notice that she never spoke during times of silence, because of the way she paid attention to whatever was said to her, the respect she showed those who broke the silence, the way she reacted to what they said with her eyes, her facial expression, her body language. There was something majestic in her being that can only be called contemplative. God was her center.

What was not obvious to anyone, however, was how behind the cloister walls she quickly lost the "sense of feeling" that once inspired her faith. She came to Carmel to find the desert, and the desert is what she found. She knelt for long hours in adoration before the Blessed Sacrament bereft of the fervor with which she used to pray. By her own account, her prayer became "nothing but drowsiness and distraction." She notes this without discouragement and seemingly without surprise. She entered Carmel with no illusions, not to find enjoyment in praying but simply to spend her whole life in prayer, come what may. If she did not expect to be coddled by the other sisters in the convent, she did not expect to be coddled by Jesus either. He was the one to be pleased. She did not expect to be emotionally rewarded for pleasing Him. Her only pleasure was in doing His Will.

Distraction and a lack of inspiration were characteristic of her prayer life through most of her life as a Carmelite. There were, of course, exceptions—occasions when she felt the joy of her love for Jesus, but these were rare. For the most part she lived in the dark night of faith and loyally plodded on. The rest of the nuns did not know this, for she kept it to herself. The final trial of faith—which she endured constantly for the last eighteen months of her life—became known to the community only after she died, when it was revealed in her writings. She did not let it be known earlier for fear it might disturb the faith of others. Despite her experience, she went on believing, saying to herself that she would gladly shed the last drop of her blood to give witness to the faith that God gave her.

What is astonishing is that an inner life that seems from one perspective bare and uneventful reflected so much outward joy. Thérèse characteristically wore a charming smile. It was completely authentic, never forced. During the time of recreation in the convent each day she was the life of the party. She was very talented in doing imitations and could cause gales of laughter in the common room. Her impersonation of a guide in Rome was riotously funny, as his Italian accent mangled the French he tried to speak. When she wasn't smiling, her face seemed always about to do so, and she was wonderful to live with. Long after she had died, the nuns often spoke of her spirit of joy. One sister who suffered from periods of depression described what Thérèse's smile meant to her. She recalled that one night during the *altum silentium,* the strict nighttime silence that began after Compline (Night Prayer) and lasted until the following day, Thérèse passed her in the corridor. Apparently sensing her despondency, Thérèse simply nodded amiably while bestowing upon her one of her most beautiful smiles. The sister recalled the incident years later: "Oh, that smile of Sister Thérèse, how it lifted the burden from my shoulders and filled my heart with joy!"

In a letter Thérèse wrote to Pauline when the latter was mother prioress, we get a glimpse of her deep spirituality in the Carmelite order. Thérèse was making a private retreat of ten days, and Pauline had slipped her a note, asking how things were going. That note has been lost, but Thérèse's reply has fortunately been preserved and deserves careful reading. She was only seventeen years old and had been less than two and a half years in the convent when she wrote it.

My own little Mamma, thank you, oh, thank you! . . . If you only knew what your letter says to my soul! . . . But the little hermit must tell you the itinerary of her trip and here it is. Before she left, her Fiancé seemed to ask her in what country she desired to travel, what route she desired to follow. . . . The little fiancée answered that she had but one desire, that of being taken to the summit of the *mountain of Love*. To reach it many routes were offered to her, and there were so many perfect ones that she saw she was incapable of choosing. Then she said to her divine guide: "You know where I want to go, You know *for whom* I want to climb the mountain, for whom I want to reach the goal. You know the one whom I love and the one whom I want to please solely; it is for Him alone that I am undertaking this journey. Lead me, then, by the paths which He loves to travel. I shall be at the height of my joy provided that He is pleased. Then Jesus took me by the hand, and He made me enter a subterranean passage where it is neither cold nor hot, where the sun does not shine, and in which the rain or the wind does not visit, a subterranean passage where I see nothing but a half-veiled light, the light which was diffused by the lowered eyes of my Fiancé's Face! . . .

My Fiancé says nothing to me, and I say nothing to Him either, except that *I love Him more than myself,* and I feel at the bottom of my heart that it is true, for I am more His than my own! . . . I don't see that we are advancing towards the summit of the mountain since our journey is being made underground, but it seems to me that we are approaching it without knowing how. The route on which I am has no consolation for me, and nevertheless it brings me all consolations since Jesus is the one who chose it, and I want to console Him alone, alone![4]

The letter ends there, except for a few pleasantries. If it is not a description of a true mystical experience, it is hard to imagine what a mystical experience might be. There is no reason to think that Pauline shared the letter with anyone. She carried

---

4   Thérèse to Sister Agnes of Jesus (Pauline), Aug. 30–31, 1890, in *Letters,* vol. 1, pp. 651–52.

a remarkable secret in her heart from then on, and she must often have looked at Thérèse with searching eyes, trying to imagine what went on within her when she was alone in prayer.

We too can only try to imagine what Thérèse's inner life was like. Seldom is the veil drawn aside for us as it is in this letter. There is, of course, the other famous letter that became Manuscript B, in which Thérèse seems to reveal her whole soul, and that letter is charged with emotion. There is also the passage in the autobiography where she describes the mystical experience that occurred when she was making the Stations of the Cross in the chapel, which left her enraptured for several days (but of which she gave no sign as she went about her daily chores).

We have only a few glimpses of her secret self and her intimacy with Jesus. As far as we know, her life was otherwise quite routine, but it was in that routine that she was able to find Him at every moment, in the prosaic here and now of life's ordinary ways. It is worth noting that even in this remarkable letter it seems apparent that she felt no exalted emotion. "The route on which I am has no consolation for me, and nevertheless it brings me all consolations since Jesus is the one who chose it, and I want to console Him alone, alone!" (*Letters,* vol. 1, p. 652).

Can we find a better description of the real Thérèse than those words as she stands as the great teacher of the value of the ordinary and makes the convincing argument that holy feelings are not what make us pleasing to God. The latter are what are called "lights on" people, and they are no more pleasing to God than those who are "lights off."

Most of us experience fervent feelings at least occasionally, and some of us do so often. The point Thérèse makes is that holy feelings do not make us holy. What makes us holy is clinging to God's Will even when the lights go off, persevering in prayer even when prayer is dry and distracted.

CHAPTER 5

Enduring Conviction

June 9, 1895, is a major date in the spiritual journey of Saint Thérèse. On that day she wrote her well-known "Act of Oblation to Merciful Love." The Act of Oblation might be called her last will and testament. In it she deeds over to God everything she possesses and everything she is—her whole self summed up, in a formal and, we might say, official document.

Thérèse had never held anything back from God, but before she died she wanted to put her gift to Him on record, sign and seal it, and solemnly state that the gift was forever. After making her Act of Oblation she lived another two years and four months. Before her, it is true, there remained the titanic struggle of her night of faith, but that long winter of her life would add nothing to her development. It was simply the final test of her absolute fidelity to God, the last living out of the Act of Oblation.

It had long been her conviction that "God is nothing but Mercy and Love." This was the foundation of all her spirituality, the rock on which for her everything rested. By its very nature God's love is merciful, and to His mercy she wished to consecrate herself solemnly. She knew of devout souls who offered themselves as victims of His justice, but she wanted no part of that kind of offering. She saw all God's attributes in the light of His mercy, even His justice—indeed, especially His justice. If He were not merciful, He would not be just. Thérèse took to heart our humanity. She was convinced that God fully appreciated not only that we are made as weak creatures, but also that it is the only way He *could* make us. If He made us perfect, He would be making another God—and there cannot be two Gods.

The idea of formulating her Act of Oblation to God's mercy came as a sudden impulse one day during Mass, and—taking her sister Céline with her— she went immediately to see the prioress. The step was too important for her to take on her own; she would do it only with the permission of her superior. The prioress at this time was her sister Pauline. Years later Céline, recalling the moment, described how Thérèse asked for permission to suffer as a holocaust of Merciful Love together with her, and gave Mother Agnes a brief explanation. She said Mother Agnes was in a hurry and did not seem to understand fully what it was all about, but granted permission for anything Thérèse wished, so thoroughly did she trust her prudence.

Pauline told her to write out the formulation and bring it back for her approval. Thérèse went to her cell to make a final draft, which she brought to Pauline, who read it and approved it. Thérèse called it the "Offering of Myself as a Victim of Holocaust to God's Merciful Love." Its opening paragraph and the two paragraphs with which it concludes contain the substance of all that she put into the full text, and these paragraphs are quoted here.

O My God, Most Blessed Trinity, I desire to *Love* You and make You *Loved,* to work for the glory of Holy Church by saving souls on earth and liberating those suffering in purgatory. I desire to accomplish Your will perfectly and to reach the degree of glory You have prepared for me in Your Kingdom. I

desire, in a word, to be a saint, but I feel my helplessness and I beg You, O my God! to be Yourself
my *Sanctity*! (*Story,* p. 276)

The words are solemn, and she wrote them with
great earnestness. The next few paragraphs spell out
her spirituality in detail, and the final two paragraphs
describe what is required and state clearly the commitment she made in reciting it. We see how vibrant
her relationship with God continued to be despite
the difficulties she was experiencing.

In order to live in one single act of perfect Love,
I OFFER MYSELF AS A VICTIM OF HOLO-
CAUST TO YOUR MERCIFUL LOVE, asking
You to consume me incessantly, allowing the waves
of *infinite tenderness* pent up within You to over-
flow into my soul, and that thus I may become a
martyr of Your *Love,* O my God!

May this martyrdom, after having prepared me
to appear before You, finally cause me to die and
may my soul take its flight without any delay into
the eternal embrace of *Your Merciful Love.*

I want, O my *Beloved,* at each beat of my heart
to renew this offering to You an infinite number of
times, until the shadows having disappeared I may

be able to tell You of my *Love* in an *Eternal Face to Face*. (*Story*, p. 277)

She signed it with her baptismal name, Marie-Françoise-Thérèse, which she no longer used after entering religious life. This Act of Oblation was a deeply personal gesture, the meaning of which should not be lost on us. It expresses her vocation—not specifically as a Carmelite nun but as a baptized Christian. There is nothing elitist about what Thérèse was doing on June 9, 1895, and nothing extreme. It was the expression of the commitment that baptism implies in making us members of the Mystical Body of Christ. We are meant, all of us, to grow into God's Holy People. Those who are baptized—the secretary or the mother of a household, the bus driver or the gas attendant, the priest or the pope or the university professor—are all meant to be mystics. There are many levels of being a mystic. You and I are never going to reach the level of Thérèse, no more than we will ever reach the level of God's most holy Mother, Mary. Somebody has to be the greatest, and that means the rest of us have to be less. In all the meadows of the world, wildflowers grow in profusion. God is the Creator of every flower in the field, and He loves each because it is His creation.

Thérèse intended the Act of Oblation to be for all of us; she did not want to make it alone. She turned to the one person who was closer to her than anyone else and understood her very deeply, her sister Céline, who was in Carmel with her as Sister Geneviève. Thérèse gave her the copy to read and invited her to make the Act with her, and Céline agreed without any hesitation. Four days later she and Céline knelt before the statue of Our Lady of the Smile, which figured in the dramatic cure of Thérèse when she was ten years old. Together they made their final commitment to God's Merciful Love.

Not long after that, Thérèse invited her oldest sister Marie to join them in the Act. Marie hesitated. She balked at the phrase "victim of holocaust," which she found intimidating. Characteristically she protested, saying that she did not want any more suffering than she already had. Thérèse explained that she would not get any more, that the Act of Oblation does not increase one's suffering. What it does is commit us to accept life lovingly as it comes to us, with the suffering that it already inevitably involves. Suffering is a natural part of everybody's life; even a baby starts life by crying. Life in this world is mingled with pain.

Marie was right to make her objection, but so was

Thérèse in giving her answer. The purpose of the Act of Oblation is not to invite God to send us more suffering. The Act, according to Thérèse, makes one a victim not of God's Justice but of His merciful love. The thought that God could be vindictive was unacceptable to her. All that He wants from us is that we allow Him to love us, and that we cast ourselves into His arms with blind confidence in His kindness. Once this was explained to Marie, she gladly joined the others and made her own Act of Oblation.

Another Marie would also make the Act of Oblation. Sister Marie of the Trinity came to Carmel when Thérèse was mistress of novices, and the two became fast friends. She was delightful, full of good will, and, like Thérèse, full of fun. The night before she entered Carmel, she went to the fair in her town and gleefully rode the carousel for a last fling. But she was a new recruit who needed seasoning before Thérèse invited her to make the Act of Oblation. When Thérèse finally broached the subject with her, young Marie at first demurred, saying she needed a long preparation before taking a step of such importance. Thérèse replied that the Act was more important than she could imagine. The only preparation in God's eyes was to humbly realize our unworthiness.

She promised that she would be with the sister when she pronounced the Act the next day in the chapel and that she should not be afraid.

Did Marie, Céline, and Marie of the Trinity become perfect after making the Act of Oblation? Of course not. They all had faults until the day they died. So did Thérèse. She was not interested in an asceticism that would make one perfect in all virtue. She was more concerned in our having ever-increasing confidence in the merciful love of God. Thérèse knew with certainty that it is the nature of God's love to come down, to bend low over us with tender affection, as a mother and father bend low over the cradle of their newborn baby, overjoyed to be his parents before he has done anything to deserve their love. They love him because he needs to be loved. This is the spirituality of Saint Thérèse, who loved her littleness, her helplessness, and wanted no more than to be the child of God, thoughtless of her merits and wanting to give herself with utter abandonment to His Love. How much she was telling us when she remarked with joy and without any hesitation that she would gladly go to God "with empty hands" (*Story*, p. 277).

Those who wish to take Saint Thérèse with full seriousness will do well to pronounce her Act of

Oblation at some point in their lives. The moment should not be rushed. Sister Marie of the Trinity was correct in seeing it as a step of grave importance, requiring serious forethought. The Act should come as the culmination of a reasonably long acquaintance with Thérèse and with her radically new approach to God. We should see the sense of it—the truly profound theology that is the bedrock on which it stands—and we should earnestly want to make it with the same beautiful freedom that characterized its author.

When we are finally ready, we should think of it as enrolling in her school of spirituality, with a peace and contentment to remain in it for the rest of our lives as we keep on growing in the wisdom with which God endowed her. The Act should mark a clear break with fear and anxiety about the past, and a conviction that every moment is a fresh beginning, with all the peace and joy her doctrine inspires. Without drama and with deep serenity, it should mark our final conversion to the truth of Jesus, who said to all His followers: "My yoke is easy, and my burden is light (Matt. 11:30); and "Behold, I make all things new" (Rev. 21:5).

The Gift of Thérèse's Little Way

There is nothing with which Thérèse is more closely identified than her Little Way. It is not exactly a teaching but simply her way of coming very close to God. It is a road to be followed, a direction to take, a means for reaching our destination. It came to her as she searched earnestly for God, wanting to love Him with her whole heart. Her love was not pious sentimentality but a real and tangible expression of her relationship with God, what she held dear from her childhood right through the desert days she encountered in the Carmelite convent. Thérèse did not formulate her radical insight. Humans love formulas, clear definitions, but Thérèse did not deal in such formalities. She came to her Little Way by intuition, and then she lived it. She was a spiritual genius, creative and original, who broke new ground. Her Little Way was, in a sense, God's priceless gift to her to share with the whole Church, for the solace and sanctification of countless millions of "little souls" like yours and mine. When she spoke of it she called it simply "my way," and she insisted that it was a sure way—and furthermore, a new way.

Much has been written about the Little Way, sometimes so much that it is difficult to appreciate the boundless possibilities that Thérèse saw. We will begin with two stories that set a different context for understanding the relevance of Thérèse's teaching for us today. They have more to do with Thérèse's Little Way than first meets the eye, and they may help us to realize the significant and minor ways we can live by her example.

The first story is about a priest from the Archdiocese of New York named Jim Conlan. Until his death in the 1990s he had an immense influence on a great many people, and he is sorely missed. Jim was a man of multiple talents with a keen interest in drama, a riveting preaching style, and an unusual capacity for making friends. He always saw the bright side of things, and he had a great way of making others feel affirmed. Jim walked with a limp as a result of suffering infantile paralysis in his childhood; the disease left him with one leg a few inches shorter than the other. The heel of one shoe was built up with a lift to make up for the difference. He was a handsome man with welcoming eyes and a face that liked to smile, and the thing about the smile was that it was gallant.

For several years he headed up the Archdiocesan Mission Band and preached in many of the local parishes. There was a story he sometimes used in preaching, and when he told it you could hear a pin drop. In his high school years at Fordham Prep, he grew painfully aware of his handicap and bitter about what it did to his life. At basketball games he sat in the stands while his classmates excelled on the court. When there was a dance, he stood on the sidelines and watched. By the age of fifteen he began to feel that life was passing him by, and he was starting to become embittered.

One day on his way home after classes, he saw a priest coming toward him on the sidewalk; he must have been a professor at the university. He was somewhat on in years, with a wiry build and a head of steel-gray hair. As they were about to pass each other, the priest grabbed Jim's arm to stop him and—with no warning—asked him a question: "What's that you have there, son, polio?"

"Yes, Father," Jim answered.

"Are you glad you have polio?" the priest followed up.

Jim froze and shot back: "No, I'm not glad I have polio!"

But the priest replied, "Let me tell you something, son. Until the day comes when you can say to God and really mean it, 'Lord, I'm glad I have polio,' you'll never amount to anything!" Without a further word the priest walked on, and Jim never saw him again.

All the way home Jim burned with resentment, and at supper that night he said hardly a word. As the evening wore on his resentment kept building. When he went to bed, he could not sleep, so he got up and sat by the window, staring at the lamppost outside. After a long time he began to cry. "I never cried like that before, a river of tears," he recalled. When he stopped crying he started to pray, and he suddenly felt God was very near. At length he found himself saying, "Lord, I'm glad I have polio," and he knew that he meant what he said.

For a while he sat there silently, trying to take in what had happened to him. Back in bed, he slept soundly for what was left of the night, and when he awoke in the morning he was a new man. In his preaching he would say that he never turned back to the boy he had been, and he would always add at the end of the story: "I know I would not be a priest today if that Jesuit had not floored me with the statement: 'Son, until the day comes when you can say to God and really mean it, *Lord, I'm glad I have polio,* you'll never amount to anything.'"

I think of this story as an example of the Little Way. What Jim did that night was put into practice Thérèse's doctrine of littleness, of joyous and whole-hearted acceptance of ourselves with all our diminishments, no matter what they are—being glad that we are who we are and have what we have. Thérèse never taught us to seek suffering. What she taught us to do was simply to love life the way it is and ourselves the way we are, to love what she called our "littleness." By this she meant our poverty, our diminishments, our failures, the things we're ashamed of and wish we could do over if we had another chance. She did not hesitate to call these our riches. When her loving father literally went out of his mind and had to be committed to what was then called an insane asylum, even though her father's illness broke her heart, she referred to the family's sufferings as "our riches."

Thérèse teaches us to accept what cannot be changed—even to welcome it as God's holy will, to be glad about it as Father Jim Conlan was glad about his polio. For Thérèse, this was a fundamental principle. The older I get, the more I see the wisdom of her teaching. A calm look back down the long years of life tells me that the things I looked upon as disasters turned out to be blessings in disguise. Without them I would not have grown but would have remained a smart aleck who thinks he is really something—instead of who I truly am. Well into my late eighties, I dare to think that some of the best qualities in me would not be there if some of the worst things had not happened to me—including, naturally, those that I caused myself.

I humbly offer one of my experiences of the Little Way. It occurred when I began my retirement and a couple of old friends planned a dinner party in their home in Connecticut to mark the occasion. I add this story not because it is comparable to Jim's acceptance of polio, but precisely because it is a seemingly minor incident in the scheme of life, yet the kind that can fill one with a strong dose of feeling inadequate.

The date for the dinner party was fixed well in advance, and some thirty people who knew me were invited. I phoned the husband the day before to tell him how grateful I was and that I planned to arrive early so as to be there when the guests arrived. By the next morning, however, when my friend, Bishop Sheridan, called to ask if I was free for dinner that night, the event slipped my mind and I answered yes. When he came to my room in St. Thomas More in New York at 6:00 p.m., we chatted pleasantly for a half hour or so, and then he asked casually, "By the way, when is that dinner for your retirement?"

I leaped to my feet, and in a panic I called my host, but at first I could reach only his answering machine. When I finally got through to him, he said three words: "Where are you?" I said I was in my room, and, sick with shame, I told him I had forgotten about the dinner—after speaking to him on the phone the day before!

I said: "John, I can't imagine how I did this. I have no excuse; maybe I'm getting Alzheimer's." (I almost wished it were so, for then I would at least have an excuse.) I said I'd jump in my car and get there as soon as possible, but he told me the drive was at least an hour and a half. The dinner would be over and the guests would have left by the time I arrived. I did not even know who the guests were; I have never inquired, and with exquisite discretion, my hosts have never told me.

I cannot describe the shame I felt. What would they all think of me when he hung up the phone and told them? And what about his wife? The next day I sent her two dozen long-stemmed roses, but what good could they do? For three days my stomach twisted in remorse. Then, out of nowhere, Jim Conlan's story came back to me. On the wall of my living room at the time was an enlarged photograph of Thérèse, one from which she looks right into your eyes. I went over and stood before it. I looked at her and said: "Thérèse, I'm glad I forgot," and I really meant what I said. I made a terrible mistake—and in accepting it I accepted my vulnerability and humanness. It was then that the anguish vanished, and a sense of peace came over me. I was still upset for my hosts, but I made my peace with the Little Way. My hosts and I have had several dinners since, and they have forgiven me with their amazing grace. We are better friends now than we ever were. This also is the Little Way.

CHAPTER 6

Living the Little Way

When Thérèse was alive, it was commonly thought that the high road to holiness was a hard one of strict asceticism, strong discipline, and demanding sacrifice. One needed a powerful will to storm the heights of such holiness—to be a "great soul," as Thérèse called such a person. This, of course, is not unlike how people today may still view the prospect of belonging to the Church—and, instead of being inspired by such a challenge, many find themselves overwhelmed, incapable of attempting to measure up in some small way.

Thérèse, within the walls of the Carmelite convent, quietly overthrew that spirituality. She realized that she was a little soul, and she also knew—and this is what is revolutionary about her—that she, and all the other little souls like her, could still be great saints. Ahead of her time, Thérèse believed in the fundamental message of Vatican II: the universal call to holiness. Little souls, who make up the vast majority of humanity, are well aware of their limitations, their frustration with even the small difficulties encountered every day, their poverty of spirit, and their inability to come close to accomplishing anything of real significance. Nonetheless, these souls can still have an intimate relationship with God, and their lives can have a meaning and legacy equal to that of the great souls. The way for them (as it was for Thérèse) is not the way of greatness but of littleness.

Gradually, we see Thérèse's understanding of this way unfolding. She would not come to a full understanding of it until her life was almost over, but early on in Carmel she accepted the small challenges before her. She had not been a Carmelite for very long when she rejected severe penance such as wearing a coarse undergarment and instead contented herself with small penances—like checking her response when someone annoyed her, showing kindness to a nun she did not like, living the rule faithfully, sitting up straight rather than slouching, or putting up graciously with the penetrating cold of Normandy winters in a monastery whose only heated place was the common room. The little things of everyday living, of which all of us have more than enough, were sufficient for Thérèse and will be sufficient for those who wish to follow her "way."

It is easy to find in her autobiography examples of what she means. She tells the story with great humor of an old nun who sat behind her in the chapel. This nun had the strange habit of scraping her false teeth with her fingernails, which nearly drove Thérèse crazy. To pray with that noise going on in back of her was impossible. She could concentrate on nothing else. She even tried to pretend it was music. But she never turned with anger in her eyes and asked the nun for pity's sake to stop.

Thérèse believed that such seemingly small sacrifices are as important as big sacrifices; that they make us as pleasing to God as big sacrifices do. She also knew that there is no one who does not have the chance to offer up such sacrifices every day. It takes a long time to master the art of this kind of asceticism, but it is doable. That's the great thing about Saint Thérèse—her spirituality is within the reach of everyone. Not that all of us will practice it with the same confidence and love that she did, but we can at least aim at practicing it well.

The first hint we have of Thérèse recognizing her

Little Way came early in her religious life when she encountered in confession a Franciscan priest named Alexis Prou. He came to the Carmel to preach a retreat to the sisters as a last-minute substitute for another priest who had a great reputation for preaching to cloistered nuns, but who took sick. Father Alexis enjoyed no such reputation. All he was known for was preaching parish missions to humble folk and bringing many sinners back to the fervent practice of their faith. Some of the sisters were disappointed, but for Thérèse he was a gift from God. She tells the story in her autobiography:

> Ordinarily, the retreats that are preached are more painful to me than the ones I make alone, but this year it was otherwise. . . . At the time I was having great interior trials of all kinds, even to the point of asking myself whether heaven really existed. I felt disposed to say nothing of my interior dispositions since I didn't know how to express them, but I had hardly entered the confessional when I felt my soul expand. After speaking only a few words, *I was understood* in a marvelous way and my soul was like a book in which this priest read better than I did myself. He launched me full sail upon the waves of *confidence and love* which so strongly attracted me,

but upon which I dared not advance. He told me that *my faults caused God no pain, and that holding as he did God's place,* he was telling me *in His name* that God was very much pleased with me.

Oh! how happy I was to hear those consoling words! Never had I heard that our faults *could not cause God any pain,* and this assurance filled me with joy, helping me to bear patiently with life's exile. I felt at the bottom of my heart that this was really so, for God is more tender than a mother. (*Story,* pp. 173–74)

The remarks with which Thérèse begins her account are very interesting. She was far from what we think of as a pious soul. She did her own thinking, and she lived in the real world of her own time. It was the time of Marx, Darwin, Freud, Nietzsche, and others who were the makers of the modern world. The frightening thought that these skeptics might be right and she might be wrong would inevitably occur to her, and she needed to talk with someone she trusted, someone who could help her with her hesitations. This wise confessor calmed the troubled waters of her faith, and as far as we know the problem about the existence of life after death did not bother her again—until it struck once more like a bolt of lightning in 1896 on Easter Sunday. It did not go away but tormented her day and night until she died a full year and a half later. But for now, she was still climbing the heights of her spiritual journey, and she was grateful to Father Alexis.

"He launched me full sail upon the waves of *confidence and love* which so strongly attracted me, but upon which I dared not advance," she wrote (*Story,* p. 174). Confidence and love are the essence of the Little Way, but she was hesitant up until this encounter with Father Alexis to feel sure of this, for fear that she was moving too quickly and perhaps going too far on her own. She needed reinforcement, and this wise and seasoned confessor gave it to her. She never forgot him for that. She was eighteen at the time and less than three years into religious life.

I like to imagine his reaction when he came across this reference to him in her autobiography. He must have glowed with pleasure as he recalled the earnest voice of an innocent young woman whose face was hidden behind the confessional screen.

CHAPTER 7

Marie's Question

It was midway during her final ten-day retreat in September 1896 that Thérèse wrote her clearest descriptions of the Little Way. She was responding to her sister, Marie, who had sent her a note wanting to know what secrets Jesus was revealing to Thérèse during her retreat and asking her to clarify in writing the "little doctrine" that the two had often discussed, but which Marie did not yet fully understand.

Already tuberculosis was winning the relentless conquest of her young body, and her soul was in the depths of the spiritual darkness of her long trial of faith. But she was at the height of her spiritual maturity, and the correspondence, which appears in Manuscript B of her autobiography, is the finest piece that she ever wrote.

One stands in awe of Thérèse's capacity to produce

such a masterpiece while she was under such physical and emotional strain. There is not the slightest hint of her frightful suffering anywhere in the manuscript. She literally takes leave of herself and becomes lost in the desire to convey the depth of God's love for her and her love for Him.

She begins by describing a dream she had just before dawn one morning about the Venerable Anne of Jesus. Mother Anne was a friend and collaborator of Saint Teresa of Avila, who began the reform of the Carmelite order in Spain in the sixteenth century. She was sent by Teresa of Avila with a few companions to found the first Carmelite convent in France, and of course was greatly revered in all the convents there, including the one in Lisieux where Thérèse lived. In her dream Thérèse asked Mother Anne if she was completely pleasing to Jesus or was there anything further that He wished from her. Embracing her fondly with a hug she never forgot, Mother Anne assured her that Jesus was delighted with her and she should simply continue on the road she was taking. Thérèse awakened at dawn profoundly consoled and full of joy. It is interesting that she did not think of this as a vision but only as a dream, yet it remained engraved on her memory in every detail and was a source of strength even in the darkest of times.

Recounting the dream in her autobiography, she then launches into the wild desires—follies, as she called them—that she was experiencing at the time. She longed to be a priest, a prophet, an apostle, a Doctor of the Church, a martyr. She wanted to experience all the martyrdoms of history and proclaim the Gospel the world over, from the beginning of human history until the end. No wonder she called these desires follies. She wanted to persuade everyone to love Jesus with the love that filled her own heart. In no way did she want these things for herself. She wanted them for His pleasure alone, because she realized how much He longs for our love. She *knew* that He thirsts for it, and that this is the ultimate meaning of His cry on the Cross: "I thirst!" She yearned to slake His thirst, and she was distressed that so many who know Him seem unaware of the passion with which He loves them—and that so many do not even know of Him.

Manuscript B concludes with the story of the "little bird," which she saw as a symbol of herself in the terrible darkness of her night of faith. She was a master of parables, and she made up some very beautiful, clear, candid, and compelling little stories. They are presented with such disarming simplicity that one can miss the depth of truth in them, particularly if we let ourselves be put off by the simplicity of her language and imagery.

In this parable, she describes a little bird that has the aspirations of an eagle but is unable to soar as the eagle can to the lofty heights of "the Divine Sun." Unworried by its weakness, it remains steadfast in its trust that beyond the clouds the Sun goes on shining. "Nothing will frighten it, neither wind nor rain, and if dark clouds come and hide the Star of Love, the little bird will not change its place because it knows that beyond the clouds its bright Sun still shines on and that its brightness is not eclipsed for a single instant" (*Story,* p. 198).

The parable is about Thérèse; she is the little bird. There is nothing trivial about the comparison, nothing childish. If we read the parable with an open mind, we will recognize the great depth of it, and we will understand why Thérèse placed such emphasis on it. It is the climax of Manuscript B.

I have read Manuscript B dozens of times during the course of my life, without ever feeling that I plumbed its depths. But in reading for the third time Conrad De Meester's new French edition of the autobiography, and with the help of his insightful notes, I finally began (in my eighties!) to have a real sense of what lies buried beneath the surface of its lyrical prose.

What I have described here provides only a bare outline of Manuscript B. One must return to it in Thérèse's autobiography and read it slowly and prayerfully to fully appreciate its beauty.

What Thérèse writes is simple but sublime, meriting the high rank it has earned among the classics of spiritual literature. Nevertheless, there is something of great importance that Manuscript B lacks. Thérèse was unaware of the effect it might have on other people until Marie called it to her attention in a second note, which she sent to Thérèse while she was still on retreat. The last thing Thérèse did on her retreat was to answer that second note of Marie's. Her answer left no more questions to ask.

CHAPTER 8

An Unfinished Symphony

When Marie read the letter from Thérèse, dated September 8, 1896 (Manuscript B), her reaction was twofold. First, she was delighted to learn of the heights her sister was scaling on her retreat. But her second reaction was one of dismay, because she felt that Thérèse was leaving her behind. Marie had no way of scaling those heights. She had none of the holy desires that were almost tearing her sister apart. Her love for Jesus could not approach that of Thérèse. She was too candid not to admit this, and she wrote Thérèse another note immediately, the burden of which was: Tell me how I can love Jesus the way you do!

Thérèse had not thought of that "objection." On the last night of the retreat, September 17, she sat down and fired off (there is no better expression) a second letter to Marie, explaining the essence of the Little Way in the boldest manner possible. She abandoned the lyrical style of the first letter and instead used the simplest declarative style one could imagine, insisting that the Little Way was not for her alone but for Marie as well, and for all those who choose to follow it.

Thérèse starts off with what sounds like indignation: "How can you ask me if it is possible for you to love God as I love Him? If you had understood the story of my little bird, you would not have asked me this question."

She goes on:

My desires for martyrdom *are nothing*; they are not what give me the unlimited confidence that I feel in my heart. They are, to tell the truth, the spiritual riches that *render one unjust,* when one rests in them with complacence and when one believes they are *something great.* . . . I really feel that it is not this at all that pleases God in my little soul; what pleases Him is *that He sees me loving my littleness* and *my poverty, the blind hope that I have in His mercy.* . . . That is my only treasure, . . . why would this treasure not be yours? . . .

Oh, dear Sister, I beg you, understand your little

girl, understand that to love Jesus, to be His *victim of love*, the weaker one is, without desires or virtues, the more suited one is for the workings of this consuming and transforming Love. . . . It is confidence and nothing but confidence that must lead us to Love.[5]

This second letter is Thérèse's last word on the Little Way. It is as plain and straightforward as human speech can be. The Little Way has nothing to do with transports of joy or lofty religious sentiments. It is for ordinary people like Marie. It is for the army of little souls whom Thérèse envisioned. When she sat down to write the letter of September 17, 1896, she was fighting with her back to the wall in defense of her doctrine and its *application to everyone*—both those with lively religious sensibilities and those without them.

Without this letter, unquestionably the final statement of Thérèse on the Little Way, Manuscript B is an unfinished symphony. This letter is the final movement, which plays with the clash of cymbals. Thérèse's voice was raised to a shout when she says

---

5   Thérèse to Sister Marie of the Sacred Heart (Marie), Sept. 17, 1896, in *Letters,* vol. 2, pp. 999–1000).

to Marie: "That is my only treasure, . . . why would this treasure not be yours?" (*Letters,* vol. 2, p. 999). This is the challenge she makes to every one of us.

Why was the letter left out of the original edition of the autobiography? Did Marie fail to show it to the five-member board who were the first editors? I think that is most unlikely, given its content. Or did she show it to them, and they declined to include it? If the latter is true, what was their reason? Could it be that the letter deals with the question of faith and works in a way that seemed too close to Martin Luther's position?

Luther concluded that we are not saved by our works, but by our faith in Jesus's sacrifice, which opens us to God's mercy. Thérèse fully agrees— but she adds a phrase: "*If* we think they are something great." Luther left that out. The life of Thérèse from beginning to end was filled with good works, and they were most pleasing to God. But she knew it was not the works that saved her. They were the consequence of her faith, and they were pleasing to God because they were the fruits of her confidence in Him. God is delighted when we *trust* Him. Often the Little Way is reduced to performing little things with fidelity. That is part of it—the asceticism of it, if you wish. But it is "confidence and nothing but confidence" that God looks for in us, to which Thérèse added the important words "that must lead us to Love." This is also part of the Little Way.

Whatever the explanation of the omission of this letter from the autobiography, I humbly and respectfully suggest that the letter of September 17, 1896, be placed in future editions of the autobiography, so all those who read it may experience the joy of its consoling reassurances.

I wish to conclude this chapter by reproducing here the last two letters between Marie and Thérèse. To read them is to understand the beautiful relationship that existed between those two sisters. We can see the importance of Marie in this process: *She is the one who forced Thérèse to write.* Manuscript A was written at her suggestion. Manuscript B was a letter to her. And Manuscript C would never have been written if Manuscript A had not been written in the first place. If it were not for Marie, we would never have heard of Thérèse, and the priceless gift of the Little Way would have been lost to the spirituality of our times. The "little godmother" performed her function admirably; the "army of little souls" owes her an immense debt of gratitude, and so does Thérèse.

Here is Marie's second letter—reacting to that part of Manuscript B addressed to Jesus.

September 17, 1896

Dear little Sister, I have read your pages burning with love for Jesus. Your little godmother is *very happy* to possess this treasure and very grateful to her dear little girl who has revealed the secrets of her soul in this way. Oh! what should I say about these lines marked with the seal of love? . . . Simply one word concerning myself. Like the young man in the Gospel, a certain feeling of sadness came over me in view of your extraordinary desires for martyrdom. That is the proof of your love; yes, you possess love, but I myself! no, never will you make me believe that I can attain this desired goal, for I dread all that you love.

This is a proof that I do not love Jesus as you do. Ah! you say you are doing nothing, that you are a poor weak little bird, but your desires, how do you reckon them? God Himself looks upon them as works.

I cannot speak to you any longer; I began this note this morning, and I have not had a minute to finish it. It is five o'clock. I would like you to tell your little godmother, in writing, if she can love Jesus as you do. But only briefly, for what I have is sufficient for my joy and my sorrow. For my joy, when I see to what a degree you are loved and privileged; for my sorrow, when I have a foreboding of the desire that Jesus has to pluck His little flower! Oh! I wanted to cry when I read these lines that are not from earth but an echo from the Heart of God. . . . Do you want me to tell you? Well, you are possessed by God, but what is called . . . absolutely possessed, just as the wicked are possessed by the devil.

I would like to be possessed, too, by good Jesus. However, I love you so much that I rejoice when seeing you are more privileged than I am.

A short note for little godmother.

(no signature; *Letters,* vol. 2, p. 997)

Here is Thérèse's vitally important letter replying to Marie's dismay.

September 17, 1896

Dear Sister, I am not embarrassed in answering you. . . . How can you ask me if it is possible for you to love God as I love Him? . . .

If you had understood the story of my little bird,

you would not have asked me this question. My desires of martyrdom *are nothing*; they are not what give me the unlimited confidence that I feel in my heart. They are, to tell the truth, the spiritual riches that *render one unjust,* when one rests in them with complacence and when one believes they are *something great.* . . . These desires are a *consolation* that Jesus grants at times to weak souls like mine (and these souls are numerous), but when He does not give this *consolation,* it is a grace of *privilege.* Recall these words of the Father: "The martyrs suffered with joy, and the King of Martyrs suffered with sadness." Yes, Jesus said: "Father, let this chalice pass away from me." Dear Sister, how can you say after this that my desires are the sign of my love? . . . Ah! I really feel that it is not this at all that pleases God in my little soul; what pleases Him is *that He sees me loving my littleness* and my *poverty, the blind hope that I have in His mercy.* . . . That is my only treasure, dear Godmother, why would this treasure not be yours? . . .

Are you not ready to suffer all that God will desire? I really know that you are ready; therefore, if you want to feel joy, to have an attraction for suffering, it is your consolation that you are seeking, since when we love a thing the pain disappears. I assure you, if we were to go to martyrdom together in the dispositions we are in now, you would have great merit, and I would have none at all, unless Jesus was pleased to change my dispositions.

Oh, dear Sister, I beg you, understand your little girl, understand that to love Jesus, to be His *victim of love,* the weaker one is, without desires or virtues, the more suited one is for the workings of this consuming and transforming Love. . . . The *desire* alone to be a victim suffices, but we must consent to remain always poor and without strength, and this is the difficulty, for: "The truly poor in spirit, where do we find him? You must look for him from afar," said the psalmist. . . . He does not say that you must look for him among great souls, but "from afar," that is to say in *lowliness,* in *nothingness.* . . . Ah! let us remain then *very far* from all that sparkles, let us love our littleness, let us love to feel nothing, then we shall be poor in spirit, and Jesus will come to look for us, and *however far* we may be, He will transform us into flames of love. . . . Oh! how I would like to be able to make you understand what I feel! . . . It is confidence and nothing but confidence that must lead us to Love. . . . Does not fear lead to Justice? . . . Since we see the *way,* let us run together. Yes, I feel it, Jesus wills to give us the same graces, He wills to give us His heaven *gratuitously.*

Oh, dear little Sister, if you do not understand me, it is because you are too great a soul . . . or rather it is because I am explaining myself poorly, for I am sure that God would not give you the desire to be POSSESSED by *Him,* by His *Merciful Love,* if He were not reserving this favor for you . . . or rather He has already given it to you, since you have given yourself to *Him,* since you *desire* to be consumed by *Him,* and since God never gives desires that He cannot realize. . . .

Nine o'clock is ringing, and I am obliged to leave you. Ah! how I would like to tell you things, but Jesus is going to make you feel all that I cannot write. . . .

I love you with all the tenderness of my GRATE-FUL *little childlike heart.*

Thérèse of the Child Jesus

rel. carm. ind.

(*Letters,* vol. 2, pp. 998–1000)

CHAPTER 9

The Present Moment

Many years ago Bishop Sheridan and I made a retreat that I shall always remember. We had the
loan of a friend's house in the Catskill Mountains,
the tapes of talks by Bishop Fulton Sheen for priests
on retreat, and the loveliest October weather one
could imagine. The sky was blue, a nip was in the
air, and the leaves were in the full glory of their
autumn colors. We set the times for Mass, for listening to the tapes, and the recitation of the Office.
The rest of the day was for reading, walks alone
through the countryside, and staying out of each
other's way.

None of the talks by Bishop Sheen mentioned
Saint Thérèse, but she was much in my thoughts
during this retreat. I felt there was something I was

meant to take home from this trip. One thing was the commitment to spend an hour each day in front of the Blessed Sacrament in prayer and meditation, which I did make a promise to do. But there was also something else that I could not pin down exactly. Hardly more than a hunch, it nevertheless persisted. Then, on the final afternoon, my walk took me down a long mountain road that emptied into the village of Windham. On the top of a knoll stood a little church, and I was drawn up the path to its door. The church was empty, but the burning sanctuary lamp told me the Blessed Sacrament was present, and I walked down the aisle to kneel for a prayer before the tabernacle. I then took a seat in a pew in the peace of a lovely moment. Slowly, words came to my mind to express what I felt Thérèse wanted me to realize. I wrote them down:

There is need of a daily effort to live in the
    present moment,
to accept myself constantly
with all my faults and all my sins,
no matter what I am or feel I am just now,
knowing that God Who never changes
accepts and loves me.

As I went back down the path to the main road, I turned for a last look at the little church and was startled to see what I had completely missed when I entered. Over the door was the name of the church: St. Theresa of the Infant Jesus. I don't know how I could have missed it. I broke into a smile, knowing that I wrote these words in this church that was named in her honor.

Ever since making that retreat I repeat those words each morning. They encourage and console me, and give me a sense of where I am in the turmoil of the day. By nature I am an anxious person, prone to worry about the past and frightened of the future. I am often in need of encouragement. These words have changed from a declaration into a prayer that keeps me attentive to the importance of the present moment. The experience remains a living memory, and the theme of the present moment has become a staple of my life. The older I get, the more central it becomes. Thérèse continues to teach me and call me back to the here and now, to be surprised by the riches the present moment holds.

In his well-known book *The Varieties of Religious Experience*, William James remarked that the truly great saints "lived at the red hot point of their own consciousness." The phrase is a good one, and I take it to mean that they lived as fully as possible in the present moment. Thérèse is one of those saints. During the final eighteen months before she died, she struggled with the relentless pain of tuberculosis, as it slowly consumed her lungs and spread to nearby organs. She suffered humiliating symptoms as well, everything from coughing up bloody mucus to chronic constipation. She was spared none of the embarrassments of dying. At the same time, she was enveloped in darkness. She had reached a point where she was confronted by despair. She was struggling to hold on to her dearest hope, that soon she would see the One she loved with all her heart, but the thought of suicide frightened her. The sisters watching her die were appalled by her suffering, and one of them asked her one day how she managed to carry on with patience, and even with good humor. Her reply was: "If I did not suffer minute by minute it would be impossible, but I see only the present moment. I forget the past and take good care not to anticipate the future." She had long ago learned that the present moment is the only place where peace and strength are found when things go seriously wrong.

Thérèse's witness to the importance of the present moment was not simply a technique for enduring pain bravely. If that was all it amounted to, she would be a great stoic but hardly a great saint. Far from being stoical, she was a person of deep feeling. She loved the present moment because it gave her much more than the strength to endure suffering. It gave her the presence of God. Thérèse's present moment is a priceless gift to us. We may never equal her grasp of it, but we can learn her principles and try our best to practice them.

In one of his sermons, Father Karl Rahner used a picturesque phrase that often comes back to me: "We live in the wretched little hut of our own existence," he said. Most of us are aware of our own wretchedness—it is hard to think of a better word for our failure to give God what He has a right to expect from us, or even to live up to our own expectations. How mediocre we are, how un-heroic and selfish, how much there is in our past that we wince to remember. Alone in our little hut, many of us could be devoured by thoughts of some of the things we have done and other things that we have failed to do. Thérèse, however, does not allow us to indulge in sad memories. She is the realist of the present moment. She writes of herself: "It seems to me that Love penetrates and surrounds me, that at each instant this Merciful Love renews me, purifies my soul and allows no trace of sin to remain." She writes elsewhere, "If I had committed all possible crimes, I would always have the same confidence. They would be like a drop of water thrown into a blazing fire."

Thérèse knew that the past can never be retrieved, and it is a waste of time to grieve over it. If we believe as she did that God is "nothing but mercy and love," we can put our sins behind us once we have sought His forgiveness, and forge past them. The deeds are part of history, but the guilt is gone even as history is gone. As for the future, only God knows what it will hold, and we may safely leave it in His hands. "The only thing we can be sure of the future is the Providence of God will rise before the sun," the great French preacher Henri Lacordaire said in one of his sermons. When tomorrow becomes today, God will be there to sustain us.

I sometimes conjure up a quaint scene. I am in my wretched little hut, feeling lonely, remembering my past life and what a poor job I have made of it. There is a knock on the door, and when I open it God is standing there smiling, asking me if He may come in. "I wish to be with you," he says, "to share this moment with you and to assure you that I have long ago forgiven all the things you have done that were wrong. I will help you to handle whatever may come in your future. I am the God of the Present Moment. My name is Yahweh, I Am Who Am. You are my child, and wherever you go and whatever happens to you I shall always be there to guard and protect you and show you the path you should take. I do not wish you to worry. I want you to love Me as I love you, now." Suddenly the moment is alight with His warm and loving presence, and there is nowhere else I want to be, no other moment I could prefer to this one. "Behold, I make all things new," He told us (Rev. 21:5). Every moment is *new*, and every day is a new day, a time for making a fresh start.

This scenario is of my own making, of course, but it is a way of symbolizing the truth of God's presence, and it comforts me. It keeps me from wanting to change places with anyone, happy to be myself and have the life that is mine—my own little hut, wretched though it may be, into which I can always welcome the God who made me and loves me. I feel sure that Thérèse would like this scenario. She, after all, reminds us that He is "nothing but mercy and love" giving us an intuition that we have no reason to mistrust and a concept of God in whom we may feel free and completely at home and in whom we may have implicit trust. Thérèse's whole life and all her teaching rest securely on her beautiful image of God.

Living in the present moment is not something we learn to do quickly. It grows slowly over time into a habit of being, and even over the course of a long lifetime we will not master the art to the degree that Thérèse did. But we may never lay hold of a working principle so fundamental and important as this, nor may we apply ourselves with the same determination and finality with which she gave herself to it. Surely we do not expect to equal her achievement but only to follow her way.

In addition to my practice of starting the day with the words that came to me in the little church in Windham, there is another set of words with which I love to conclude my morning prayer. They are attributed to the other Teresa, the foundress of the great reform of the Carmelite order in the sixteenth century. It was her name that was given to Thérèse in baptism.

Whoever possesses the present moment possesses
  God
Therefore whoever possesses the present moment
  possesses everything

The present moment is enough
Don't let anything trouble you.

These words were embroidered on a pillow by a friend. They need to be recited slowly, with an earnest effort to see and savor the wisdom each line contains. One may say them for years without ever exhausting their meaning. There is a subtle power in them that will sustain us and keep us growing in the love of God. They may well be inscribed in gilded letters on the wall of the little hut in which we spend our lifetime.

I began each section of this book by sharing something personal of what Thérèse has meant in my life.
I would like it to end with another story. It is about
one of those sensitive issues we tend to keep to ourselves when we are young, and yet, by my age, we
share more freely. Why I chose it for the Afterword
will become clear.

The story goes back to the early days of my priesthood. My first assignment after my ordination
in 1945 was the huge parish of St. Helena in the
Bronx, New York, where 13,000 people attended
Sunday Mass, 4,600 children crowded the grammar
and high schools, eighty-six sisters and twenty-four
brothers taught them, and four young priests served
the parish with an elderly pastor who put in longer
hours than all four of us together. The place was
a beehive of activity. The assignment was one for
which any young priest would give his right arm. I

hoped I would stay in it until I became a pastor my-self. The experience remains the honeymoon of my priesthood.

However, after two years I was invited to join the Archdiocesan Mission Band, and I leapt at the op-portunity. Preaching parish missions was exciting work: reaching out for converts, helping lapsed Cath-olics come back to the practice of their faith, and encouraging those who had never stopped practicing their faith to do so more fervently. How could I say no to such an offer?

From the vibrancy of St. Helena's I moved down-town to an old brownstone on the Lower East Side, which was the headquarters of the band. Lent was just beginning, and the six other priests were away on a mission. This left me entirely alone for the seven weeks until Easter. During that time I was to write a set of long, serious talks for my first mission. The change of pace was abrupt. At the age of twenty-eight, living on the top floor of an empty building, I was desperately lonely, and I began losing all sense of confidence. This quickly manifested itself in a writer's block. The talks I ground out were hope-lessly dull. I kept tearing them up and starting over.

Preaching was never easy for me. I always entered the pulpit fearing the worst. More often than not, I would have to write out my sermons beforehand and then, as I stood before the parishioners, I would try to become engaged by looking at them individually in the eye. This helped to keep my fears at bay. But my fears only increased during those seven weeks when there were no eyes to glance into, and my doubts had plenty of time to grow. It was seven weeks straight of stage fright. No matter how much I tried, I could not shake the tension that had overtaken me.

Longing for the sound of voices, I could hardly wait for the others to return. When the other priests finally began arriving, I could not have been happier. They were wonderful men, a good bit older than I— who, after seven weeks of missions without a moment off, were in the mood to celebrate. So was I. They welcomed me heartily and made me feel at home. They were full of stories about the missions they had just given, and the house lit up with their laughter.

But Saturday came all too quickly. It was time to head off with one of the other priests to a mission on Staten Island and deliver the sermons I had been working on for the last month and a half. My day of reckoning had arrived. I was not at all confident of the talks that were packed in my bag. I shudder to remember the opening service at which I was the preacher, for it proved to be a major disaster. My companion had the Question Box and led the Rosary, while I paced nervously up and down in the sacristy, waiting to go out for the sermon.

As I approached the pulpit, I was seized with a full-scale panic attack. My heart pounded, my palms were covered with cold sweat, and my voice locked in my throat. I could not look anybody in the eye. The rules of the Mission Band did not permit notes in the pulpit, and my memory jammed, as it searched frantically back and forth through the text I had written. How I lasted the required thirty-five minutes I shall never know.

I don't recall a word of the conversation afterward in the rectory. All I remember is that my performance was not mentioned. Bewildered and ashamed, I went to my room and got into bed. I could not sleep, but went over and over the horrid memory of what had happened in the pulpit, lamenting that I had left the parish in the Bronx where I had been well adjusted and happy, and had many friends.

This description may seem exaggerated, but believe me, what happened was all too real, and it could not have escaped the notice of the congregation. If the panic had subsided with that one episode, it would not have been so bad—just something to be forgotten or made into a comical story. But it did not subside. Every time I approached the pulpit, it returned. By Thursday night I was beside myself. I knelt by the side of my bed to say my night prayers with tears rolling down my face. Looking ahead I could see a nervous breakdown looming. In despair I turned to Saint Thérèse and begged for her help. I asked for a sign that I would somehow weather this storm. Unable to think of any other sign, I asked her to send me flowers—which may seem silly to someone reading this, but in my desperation it was all I could conceive. Few things could be more alarming for a priest than a series of panic attacks in the pulpit. It could end one's career as an active priest.

After a couple of hours of restless sleep I arose groggy at five-thirty and dragged myself over to the church for the six o'clock Mass. The women making the mission were waiting impatiently for Tony, the old Italian sacristan, to arrive and open the door. I saw him coming over the hill and down the street, with the sunrise at his back and a smile on his face. In his hand was a bunch of flowers. "I'm sorry I'm late," he said. "Coming out of my house, I saw these beautiful flowers, and I had to pick them for you."

If this sounds like the perfect end of the story, it was not. Still preoccupied and anxious from the week's experience, I ungraciously took the flowers and put them down in the sacristy and forgot about them. I was more concerned with preparing to say Mass. But several hours later the full significance of Tony's gesture hit me, and I felt worse than ever. I had been so preoccupied that I missed the gift. My mood darkened, and my fears grew about my ability to preach that evening. I was in a terrible state until about 10:00 a.m., when there was a knock on the door and the other priest from the mission walked in. "These are for you," he said, as he handed me a small bunch of lily of the valley flowers, wrapped in waxed paper. Apparently someone in the office had brought them in and given them to the priest, who in turn offered them to me. The gesture was all the more meaningful because I was well aware that lily of the valley was Thérèse's favorite flower.

That moment is carved in my memory. If I should live to be a thousand I would still remember it, and I would still believe it was Thérèse who prompted Tony to cut those flowers from his garden and bring them to me. And it was Thérèse who kindly gave me a second chance with another bouquet. Some might say this is superstition. I know in my heart it is not. I got through that nightmare of a crisis and went on to spend eight happy years as part of the Mission Band.

I do not mean to imply that panic attacks in preaching never bothered me again. From time to time they did, but I never again experienced the absolute fright I endured on that first mission. Nothing banished the threat of my neurotic problem completely, not even psychotherapy, but I have been able to cope with it. I did not pray to Thérèse to be free of nervousness forever; I only asked her to get me through that terrifying crisis. I need not add that I never walk into a pulpit without a quick prayer for calm composure.

You can understand what a shock it was in 1955 to be appointed to the faculty of our seminary as professor of homiletics—to teach, of all subjects, preaching. The three years I had that responsibility were hard ones, yet I think I was able to give the young men some simple basics from my own experience. I encouraged them to use the same voice in the pulpit as they used at the breakfast table; to enliven their talks with a good story or two but to keep them brief and to the point; to speak loud enough to be heard but never to shout, and not to speak too fast; to avoid dropping their voice at the end of a sentence, thereby letting the final words be lost; and, very important, always to deliver speech units in a single breath. Such things and a hundred others as obvious are the simple meat and potatoes of public speaking. Not to observe them destroys one's effectiveness in the pulpit.

But above all, I think I helped the seminarians to overcome their nervousness. It is, after all, normal to be a bit tense. Only one person is in the pulpit and hundreds are in the pews, and the advantage belongs to the latter. But out-and-out panic attacks are not normal—they are neurotic.

One does not forget an answer to prayer as dramatic as the one Saint Thérèse gave me on my first mission. In all the years since, she has remained the closest of friends. But there is more to friendship than favors, and I would never want to imply that a tangible answer to a prayer is an indication of anything special on my part. If we stop for a moment, I think we will realize that each of us, more often than not, has been the beneficiary of divine gifts. It may have been in the form of the kindness of an old friend or a stranger, a simple realization, an understanding, or a calm acceptance. In any case, what has bound me forever to Thérèse is not the many favors she has granted me but the truth she has taught me. That truth is the Little Way.

On a table, near the door of my room, beautifully framed and artfully scripted, are words that sum up what she sent in her letters to Maurice Bellière, a very fortunate missionary who became her "little brother." In the frame is a copy of a photograph taken of her not long before her fifteenth birthday. It is a stunning picture, and her words are even more stunning:

I am your sister and your friend,
and I will always watch over you.

I believe she says the same words to me, and will say them to anyone who takes the trouble to make her acquaintance. My hope in writing this book is that by sharing these gifts of Thérèse that graced my life, your acquaintance with her will grow into a rich and lifelong mutual relationship.